TEACHER

Bible Readers Series

A Study of Galatians

SET FREE BY GOD'S GRACE

Douglas Wingeier

Abingdon Press / Nashville

Set Free by God's Grace
A Study of Galatians

Copyright © 1993 by Cokesbury.
Abingdon Press edition published 2003.

Scripture quotations in this publication, unless otherwise indicated, are from the New Revised Standard Version of the Bible, copyrighted © 1989 by the Division of Christian Education of the National Council of the Churches of Christ in the United States of America, and are used by permission.

Lessons are based on the International Sunday School Lessons for Christian Teaching, copyright © 1990, by the Committee on the Uniform Series. Text excerpted from *Adult Bible Studies Teacher,* Spring 1994.

This book is printed on acid-free, elemental chlorine-free paper.

ISBN 0-687-02035-2

03 04 05 06 07 08 09 10 11 12—10 9 8 7 6 5 4 3 2 1
Manufactured in the United States of America.

CONTENTS

Galatians: A Letter of Admonition *5*

1. Delivered From Bondage *11*

2. Adopted as God's Children *17*

3. Freed to Grow *23*

4. Enabled to Bear Fruit *29*

5. Challenged to Love *35*

GALATIANS: A LETTER OF ADMONITION

BY LINDA OWEN

In approximately 285 B.C., the Celts migrated from Europe into central Asia Minor. These barbarian tribes overran the peninsula, levied tribute on cities and kings, and hired themselves out as mercenary soldiers. Gradually Greek kings pushed them into the central highlands of Anatolia, where they established themselves in the region of Ancyra (modern Ankara). Later, during the Roman conquests, the territory of Galatia was annexed to the Empire; and in 25 B.C., Galatia was expanded to become a Roman province under Augustus. Included in the expansion were several districts in southern Asia Minor: Pisidia and parts of Lycaonia and Phyrgia.[1] In Paul's time, the Roman province included a large area of central Asia Minor (modern Turkey). Many residents were ethnic Greeks.

Letter to Galatian Churches

Because Paul's epistle to the Galatians was not addressed to any particular churches, it is impossible to be certain whether the churches of Galatia were located in the traditional territory of the ethnic Galatians ("North Galatia") or in the expanded Roman province of Galatia ("South Galatia"). The commonly held belief among scholars is that the letter was written to churches established during Paul's first missionary journey, which were all in cities (Antioch of Pisidia, Iconium, Lystra, and Derbe) in the southern part of the Roman province (Acts 13:14–14:24). Other commentators theorize that Paul was addressing the churches founded in "North Galatia" during the second missionary journey (Acts 16:6) and later visited a second time (Acts 18:23). The letter itself gives few specifics, except that Paul had visited the churches at least once, and perhaps twice, before writing the pastoral letter (Galatians 1:8; 4:13-15). There is insufficient information to resolve the issue completely.

Dating the epistle is likewise difficult. The only certainty is that the letter must have been written after the events described in Galatians 2:1-14. In the letter Paul mentions two visits to Jerusalem (Galatians 1:18; 2:1), but Acts records five visits (Acts 9:26; 11:27-30 and 12:25; 15:1-4; 18:22; 21:17-18). Probably Galatians 1:18 and Acts 9:26 document Paul's first visit to Jerusalem after his conversion (A.D. 35); and Acts 15:1-29 and Galatians 2:1-10 record his meeting with the Jerusalem Council (dated 48 or 49). If so, the epistle may have been written as early as 48 or during the eighteen months Paul spent in Corinth in 50–51 (Acts 18:11). Another theory is that Paul wrote Galatians while he was in Ephesus (Acts 19:1–20:1), about 53–55, perhaps near the same time as writing Second Corinthians to another troubled congregation.

Paul's epistle is clear about two points, however: The churches of Galatia were churches Paul had founded (Galatians 1:8-9; 4:8-11), and the letter is addressed primarily to Gentiles converted from paganism (4:8; 5:2; 6:12).

Paul's Conversion (Acts 9)

Saul of Tarsus (Paul was his Roman name.) was of pure Jewish descent (Philippians 3:5) and a Roman citizen (Acts 23:6). As a well-educated Pharisee, he was dedicated to the outward observance of the law of Moses and affirmed it as "the embodiment of knowledge and truth," the one sure guide to God's will (Romans 2:17-20). Before his conversion, Paul regarded the church's claims about a Messiah who was crucified as blasphemy and the gospel as a scandal. Known far and wide as a zealous inquisitor and persecutor, Paul caused havoc in the church (Acts 8:3) as he sought to destroy the Christian faith.

When Stephen was stoned by a mob after being condemned by the Sanhedrin, Paul is described as approving of his death (Acts 8:1). Undoubtedly, Paul was more than an onlooker; for witnesses laid their clothes at his feet as if he were in a position of authority (Acts 7:58). After that, Paul continued the persecutions on a large scale. Christians were scourged in the synagogues, cruelly dragged from their homes, and put into prison (Acts 8:3; 22:4; 26:11). Since Paul admitted his fervor in punishing both women and men (Acts 8:3; Galatians 1:13; 1 Timothy 1:13), we may infer that many of them may have been put to death, as Stephen was.

While traveling to Damascus to bring back Christians in chains to Jerusalem, Paul was blinded by light from heaven; and he heard Christ's voice asking, "Why do you persecute me?" (Acts 9:4). Afterward, unable to see, Paul was led into the city where a follower of Jesus delivered God's message: Paul had been chosen as a missionary to the Gentiles (Acts 9:15). As the darkness fell from his eyes, Paul came face to face with "the truth of the gospel" (Galatians 2:5, 14). Paul confessed Jesus as Lord and was baptized.

At first, when Paul began proclaiming Jesus as the true Messiah, who took priority over the Temple and the law, believers were understandably suspicious. Soon the man known for his frenzied persecution of Christians became known for his intense dedication to the gospel, not the law. He committed himself to God's divine mission by traveling to much of the known world.

The Doctrine of Grace

Paul's doctrine of grace was derived from his own conversion experience on the Damascus Road (Acts 9:3-19a; 22:6-21; 26:12-23). When Paul encountered Christ, he realized that his pursuit of Christians had been a persecution of Jesus himself (Act 9:4). Dealing with what he had done in ignorance could not have been easy for Paul. As a persecutor of the church, Paul considered himself the worst of sinners (1 Timothy 1:15) and "unfit to be called an apostle" (1 Corinthians 15:9). He realized that nothing done by his own power would make him worthy of salvation. Yet his vision clarified that Jesus had died for all sinners and those who believed in him would have eternal life (1 Timothy 1:15-16). Paul was justified through faith in God's gracious gift in Christ.

Paul referred to his encounter with the living Lord as the beginning of his new life in Christ (1 Corinthians 9:1; 15:8; Galatians 1:15-16). Like himself, Paul saw the true people of God as "a new creation" (Galatians 6:15), justified by faith and not by works of the law (Galatians 3:2). He no longer regarded obedience to

the Torah as the way to righteousness, for "then Christ died for nothing" (Galatians 2:21).

After his conversion, Paul did not continue to presume that God's special relationship with the Jews excluded the Gentiles. Instead, he believed that although God's promise was made to Abraham, "the ancestor of all who believe" (Romans 4:11), Abraham's true descendants live by faith as he did. Paul maintained that anyone could be saved "through the redemption that is in Christ Jesus" (Romans 3:24).

Paul's First Mission to Galatia (Acts 13–14)

Whenever Paul entered a new town, he first went to the synagogues and shared the gospel on the sabbath day. Usually his message caused a division in the synagogue. After being rejected by the synagogue, he sought a Gentile audience.

In Antioch of Pisidia, the Jews responded with enthusiasm to Paul's preaching—until he proclaimed God's grace to the Gentiles as well. Run out of town by a mob, Paul and his companion Barnabas traveled to Iconium, a commercial center on the road between Asia and Syria. Although converts were made, Paul and Barnabas heard about a plot to stone them; so they fled to Lystra, a Roman colony to the south.

In Lystra, as Paul preached, Jewish agitators from Antioch and Iconium arrived and turned the crowd against him. This time they stoned Paul and dragged him out of the city, leaving him for dead.

The next day Paul and Barnabas traveled to Derbe, a border town. After preaching the good news there and making many disciples, they bravely returned to Lystra, Iconium, and Antioch in order to encourage the new believers. Paul and Barnabas also appointed elders in every church before continuing their missionary work outside Galatia.

Purpose of the Galatian Letter

When Paul left Galatia, he believed the fledgling churches were running well (Galatians 5:7). The pagans had accepted the gospel joyfully (4:14-15), been baptized (3:26-28), and received an outpouring of the Holy Spirit (3:2-5; 4:6).

Sometime after that, however, other itinerant missionaries arrived and began to undermine Paul's teachings. These missionaries advocated that Gentile congregations adopt Jewish rites and practices in order to assure themselves a place among the people of God. Apparently these troublemakers convinced the Galatians that Paul had failed to instruct them properly (Galatians 1:6; 3:1; 4:21; 5:4; 5:7), and Gentile Christians were already adopting some aspects of Jewish observance outlined in the Torah (4:10-11).

Outraged that the Galatians were accepting this perversion of the gospel (Galatians 1:7), Paul composed a fiery letter that stated his case for the gospel of grace. As was the custom, this epistle would have been circulated to each of the congregations, where it would have been read aloud. Undoubtedly, by writing the letter, Paul hoped to prevent defection among Christian converts and to vindicate himself against the charges of the Judaizing party.

Although the identity of Paul's rivals is unknown, it is important to recognize that they were not non-Christian Jews trying to induce the Galatians to abandon their newfound Christian faith. Instead, they were Jewish Christians who believed Jesus to be the Messiah. These Judaizers (from the verb *Judaize* [Galatians 2:14; RSV, "live like a Jew"]) saw themselves as summoning Gentiles in the name of Jesus to obey the law. Because it was given to Moses by God, they stressed obedience to everything written in the Torah (Galatians 3:10), including observance of Jewish sabbaths and feast days (Galatians 4:8-11) and the necessity of circumcision as a means of entering into a covenant relationship with the God of Israel (Galatians 5:2-4; 6:12-13; also see Genesis 17:9-14). They also promised that keeping the commandments assured salvation (Galatians 3:12).

Paul refuted their message, arguing that his rivals were preaching a false gospel: (1) Their emphasis on observance of the law as the condition for covenant membership negated the sufficiency of God's grace, which was revealed through the death of Jesus (Galatians 2:20-21). (2) Their insistence on a written code to direct and restrain believers from sin ignored the Holy Spirit, which could empower Christians to resist the desires of the flesh (Galatians 5:16-26). By thinking that the law would continue to provide the fundamental structure for the identity of the people of God, the agitators were denying the truth of the gospel, undermining the spread of Christianity, and causing disunity between Jewish and Gentile Christians.

In his emotional letter, Paul attacked not only the group of troublemakers (Galatians 1:7; 5:12) but also the believers who had abandoned the gospel (1:6). Feeling that he had wasted his efforts on the fickle Galatians (4:11) and that they had fallen from grace (5:4), Paul expressed astonishment (1:6), fear of failure (4:11), pain and perplexity (4:19-20). Sometimes he warned them (that is, against envy and conceit and disharmony [5:15]); at other times his response was scathing. He called his readers deserters (1:6), foolish, and bewitched, which implies "controlled by Satan"[2] (3:1).

At times Paul cursed the Judaizers. He warned of God's punishment, saying that they should be eternally condemned (Galatians 1:8-9; 5:10). He suggested that they castrate themselves (5:12), for in the Torah such mutilation was a cause for excommunication (Deuteronomy 23:1)—something harshly appropriate for those who had "cut off" the Galatians from Christ by overemphasizing "the cutting of flesh." He also made two accusations against his opponents: (1) They were more interested in proselytizing and promoting circumcision than in what happened to the proselytes. (2) They were ignoring other Jewish laws in order to promote circumcision (Galatians 6:12-13).

In spite of Paul's anger and frustration, his concern is evident as he urged his readers to return to Christ that they might be recipients of God's grace, offered freely in Christ.

The Crucial Problem of Circumcision

The earliest Christians were Jews who struggled with a dual identity. Their Jewishness compelled them to be strict followers of the law, but their newfound faith meant receiving salvation by faith in Christ.

For centuries Jews had been conditioned to see themselves as "God's chosen people." Traditionally, foreign believers (proselytes)—who sought the full privileges and blessings of the covenant—had proclaimed YHWH as the only God and practiced circumcision. As Christianity grew, Jewish Christians were quite willing for Gentiles to come into the church—if they first became Jews. Thus, they insisted that Gentiles be circumcised and observe the whole law of Moses, just as proselytes had done for centuries.

Many of the Gentiles, however, were men like Titus, a Greek believer who was closely associated with Paul's ministry. Undoubtedly Titus did not feel compelled to be circumcised. He appeared with Paul before the leaders of the church while the controversial issue was debated. As a living example of what Christ was doing among the Gentiles (Galatians 2:1-3), Titus and others like him were cultural descendants of Aristotle, not of Abraham. Taught by Paul that God's salvation was offered to all believers regardless of race or nationality, Titus did not understand why he must become a Jew when he had already been circumcised by baptism and the Spirit (1 Corinthians 12:13). In this he represented the view of most non-Jewish Christians.

Another major issue was whether Christians should obey Jewish laws of ritual purity and diet, which included not even eating with Gentiles. Furthermore, the observant Jew could have no dialogue with Gentiles and could not do business with them. Thus, another problem: To what extent could Jews and Gentiles associate with one another in the church?

The solution to this controversy was not easy. Paul needed to preserve the gospel and to achieve unity in the church by getting Jewish Christians to see that they too were being saved by grace. At the same time, Paul had to demolish centuries of anti-Gentile prejudice and to answer charges that he had watered down the gospel to make the Kingdom easily accessible to Gentiles. After several confrontations with Judaizers, Paul and Barnabas took their case to the council in Jerusalem (Acts 15).

There, before the church leaders—including all the apostles and elders—Paul and Barnabas reported on the miracles God had done among the Gentiles by the outpouring of the Spirit. Opposing them was a faction of Pharisees who sought to prevent the desecration of the law by having the Gentiles circumcised. This debate could have split the church. If the theological split had prevailed, the Christian movement would have become nothing other than a sect of Judaism.

In the end, the council made the decision that there should be no difference between Jews and Gentiles. The council endorsed Paul's law-free doctrine of grace by sending a letter—a charter of freedom for the Gentiles—with delegates who accompanied Paul and Barnabas back to Antioch (Acts 15:22-29). Although Gentile believers need not be circumcised, the letter specified that they should refrain from eating meat sacrificed to idols; from sexual immorality; and also from eating unbled meat of strangled animals, which reflected Torah teachings (Leviticus 17:14).

A few years later Paul circumcised Timothy, another Greek disciple (Act 16:3); but Timothy had a Jewish mother and hence he was a Jew. Paul never insisted that Jews should cease being Jews, only that Gentiles did not need to be observant Jews in order to be included among the people of God.

Problems Continue

Although the circumcision issue was settled by the Jerusalem Council, problems continued because it had not been decided whether Jewish and Gentile Christians could eat together. Later, some Jewish Christians arrived in Antioch, where the Gentile church was based, and pressured Paul's associates about sharing meals with Gentile members. Unable to withstand the pressure, Peter and Barnabas segregated themselves—much to Paul's disdain (Galatians 2:11-14). Few things could have hurt the feelings of the Gentiles more than the spiritual snobbery of refusing to eat with them. The unity inherent in baptism and the Lord's Supper could not be maintained amid the spirit of division.

Also, Paul's letters report that troublemakers continued to plague the churches. Eighteen months after Paul left Corinth, believers split into various cliques, each declaring allegiance to their favorite teacher (1 Corinthians 1:10-13; 4:6-7). Although Paul wrote a letter restating his teachings, problems escalated. In a second letter, written about 55–57, Paul was forced to defend his qualifications as an apostle (as in Galatians 1:10–2:21); this time "false teachers" in Corinth denied his authority and slandered him (2 Corinthians 2:12–3:6; 11:4-6). Also, from remarks in Romans, written about 57, we might infer that Judaizers got to Rome before Paul and discredited his gospel before he could travel there (Romans 3:8, 31). In Philippians (probably written from Rome during Paul's imprisonment in 61), Paul was still contending with Jewish Christians from Asia Minor who insisted on circumcision (Philippians 3:2-21).

We have to wonder why these Christians were so easily swayed and confused. In Galatia, the Celts had had little religion of their own and had easily adopted the superstitions and mythology of the Greeks. Under the Romans, inhabitants everywhere worshiped "savior-gods," who protected the Empire. After burning incense before the emperor's statue, worshipers were free under Roman "tolerance" to adopt any other legal religion. Whether salvation was offered in the name of the ancient gods of Greece or the emperor of Rome, people were familiar with cultic observances that promised the favor of the deity.

Thus, Gentile Christians, who were accustomed to cultic rites to win the favor of their gods, could have been led astray easily by the Judaizers' focus on the Torah. New believers would have missed the sense of assurance that they formerly derived from obedience to the law of the cult. Doubtless the Galatians wanted to grow in their Christian lives, but they were misled into believing that faith in Christ was not enough.

The Status of Torah Today

Paul's letter to the Galatians boldly declared the freedom of the Christian from slavery to sin and the law. Paul was not saying that the law is bad; in another letter he wrote, "The law is holy" (Romans 7:12). Instead, Paul was saying that the law can never make us acceptable to God. The Torah is good in that it helps us to recognize our sin and gives us an opportunity to ask for forgiveness. The law cannot possibly save us, but it gives us standards for our behavior and can guide us to live as God requires.

Although Paul expected virtuous Christian conduct and expressed his concerns about ethics, he was never legalistic. In his letters he listed vices (1 Corinthians 5; 2 Corinthians 12:20-21; Galatians 5:19-21; Ephesians 4:17-19; Colossians 3:5-11; and others), but he also listed good qualities that are by-products of the Spirit (Galatians 5:22-23; Philippians 4:8; Colossians 3:12-14). As Christians, we find the ultimate standard of Christian conduct in Christ, who gave himself for others (Philippians 2:1-11). As reconciled believers, we are called to embrace a new lifestyle motivated by the Spirit rather than by the law.

[1] From *Galatians,* by Charles B. Cousar, in the Interpretation Series (John Knox Press, 1982); page 3.

[2] From *Paul, In Other Words,* by Jerome H. Neyrey (Westminster/John Knox Press, 1990); pages 183–84.

LINDA OWEN is a former pastor, now dedicated to a full-time writing ministry. She teaches an adult Sunday school class at University United Methodist Church in San Antonio, Texas.

Adapted from *Adult Bible Studies Teacher,* March-April-May, 2002. Copyright © 2001 by Cokesbury.

Chapter One

DELIVERED FROM BONDAGE

PURPOSE

To challenge us to live in the freedom that the gospel of Christ offers

BIBLE PASSAGE

Galatians 1:6-7; 2:11-21
Background: Galatians 1–2

> ### CORE VERSES
> I have been crucified with Christ; and it is no longer I who live, but it is Christ who lives in me. And the life I now live in the flesh I live by faith in the Son of God, who loved me and gave himself for me.
> (Galatians 2:19b-20)

GET READY

Pray for the Spirit's illumination as you study a letter that has been called the "Magna Carta of Christian freedom," the "charter of evangelical faith," and the trumpet with which Martin Luther blew the reveille of the Protestant Reformation.[1] Also pray that God will help your class members bring the message of Galatians to bear on their lives.

Read through this teacher's guide to see how the five sessions flow from one another; then concentrate on this first session, Galatians 1 and 2, and what Bible commentaries have to say about the printed verses. Also look up the articles on "Freedom" in a Bible dictionary, if possible. Write your own definition of "freedom," or bring a dictionary definition to the session.

BIBLE BACKGROUND

This letter is addressed "to the churches of Galatia" (Galatians 1:2), an area that today is in western Turkey, north of Cyprus. Galatians was a circular letter, intended to be passed along to several churches. Paul founded some of these churches (in Iconium [eye-KOH-nee-uhm], Lystra [LIS-truh], Derbe [DUHR-bee], and Antioch of Pisidia [pi-SID-ee-uh]—see Acts 13:13–14:23) on his first missionary journey. Others were possibly established on his second journey (Acts 16:6) and visited on his third (Acts 18:23). All were facing the same question: Must Gentile converts abide by the ceremonial law of Judaism, including circumcision and dietary practices; or are all Christians—both Jew and Gentile—freed by Christ to live by grace?

The immediate occasion for the letter was the teaching of some troublemakers (Galatians 1:7) who were confusing believers by proclaiming a message contrary to Paul's teaching of salvation by grace through faith. These persons were probably Judaizers, Jewish Christians who insisted that male Gentiles had to be circumcised to enter the church (Galatians 6:12-13). Paul's opponents also attempted to undercut his teaching by denying his apostolic credentials.

Whether Paul was writing after his first or second journey is not certain; but the controversy had arisen after his departure, and he wrote with urgency to straighten it out and to clear his name.

Paul believed that it was wrong to keep Christianity confined as a sect of Judaism and that freedom from the law was essential to the growth of the faith among the pagan population. In stating his argument, he developed the central themes of his overall message: justification by faith, new life in Christ, the expression of love, the tension between law and freedom, the Crucifixion, the inclusiveness of the church, and the Spirit.

Paul also gave some details that expanded on the story in Acts: his previous life as a faithful Jew and his persecution of Christians (Galatians 1:13-14); his conversion and call (1:15-16); his two trips to Jerusalem (1:18; 2:1); and his physical infirmity (4:13). Interesting aspects of the organization of the early church were mentioned: The Jerusalem apostles included Cephas (Peter), James the brother of Jesus, and John (1:18-19; 2:9); a church council was called (2:1-10); the mission field was divided between Jews and Gentiles (2:9); and Peter and Paul were in disagreement (2:11-14).

The Letter to the Galatians reveals the early church in formation. The power of the gospel motivated evangelistic outreach, which provoked controversy and confrontation, which required consultation, which prompted the development of basic doctrine as we still know it today. This process, while definitive then, continues to this day as our understanding of the faith grows in response to the dialogue between the gospel and today's issues.

The epistle may be outlined as follows:

(A) Greeting and Reason for Writing (Galatians 1:1-10)
(B) Defense of Apostolic Authority (1:11–2:10)
(C) Defense of Apostolic Message (2:11–3:18)
   (1) Life by Faith, Not Works (2:11-21)
   (2) Proof of the Gospel From Experience and Scripture (3:1-18)
(D) Purpose of the Law (3:19–4:7)
(E) Freedom in Christ (4:8–6:10)
   (1) Appeals to Experience and Scripture (4:8-30)
   (2) Call to Remain Free (4:31–5:1)
   (3) Faith Expressed in Love (5:2-15)
   (4) Life in the Spirit, Not Flesh (5:16-26)
   (5) Life in the Community (6:1-10)
(F) Final Advice and Blessing (6:11-18)

We now turn to our Bible Passage.

Galatians 1:6-7. These verses state the reason for the letter. Paul was upset that false teachers were leading astray those he had brought to Christ. Paul forgot about his usual friendly thanksgiving (Romans 1:8-15; 1 Corinthians 1:4-9), expressed astonishment at the Galatians' rapid reversal, and got right to the point: There is only one true gospel, and its message should not be distorted for reasons of missionary strategy. One may adapt the approach (1 Corinthians 9:20-23)

but not the truth. Those who had done so were to be condemned (Galatians 1:8-9).

Galatians 2:11-14. After defending his apostolic status and describing his two trips to Jerusalem, Paul moved to describe his more recent encounter with Cephas (Peter) in Antioch. Peter discovered there an integrated church of Jewish and Gentile Christians worshiping and eating together, contrary to Jewish law, and at first readily participated with them. When Judaizers representing James came from Jerusalem, however, fear of their criticism caused Peter to back off. Other Jewish Christians, including even Barnabas, likewise acted insincerely. Paul confronted their hypocrisy. Peter had accepted Gentiles as equals; but here, under pressure, he retreated from "the truth of the gospel" that in Christ all persons, regardless of racial or religious origin, are free and equal. The action of Peter and others created a separation in the community and introduced a standard other than God's grace for determining Christian unity and faithfulness. By recalling this event, Paul was actually challenging the Galatians about their own inconsistency, hypocrisy, and betrayal of God's freedom and universal acceptance.

Galatians 2:15-21. These verses set forth the key argument of this letter and of all Paul's teaching: We are justified (made right with God), not by keeping the law, engaging in right conduct, or performing good works, but solely through faith in Christ. The Galatians must not compromise this principle.

Verse 15. Paul was born a Jew, like Peter and the others. Yet, even though Gentiles were automatically viewed as sinners because they were outside the law, he—like Peter and the others—was as much a sinner and as much in need of salvation as they (Philippians 3:4b-11).

Verse 16. Whether one was inside or outside the Israelite covenant was not the issue. None can be righteous in God's sight except through faith in Christ's redemptive act on the cross. Paul was here alluding to Psalm 143:2, which acknowledged that no person on earth could be righteous before the Holy One. He introduced the key concepts—*justification* and *faith* opposed to *works*—that would form the basis for his argument in the rest of the letter (Galatians 3:8, 11, 14; 5:4) and in the later and more fully developed Epistle to the Romans.

Verse 17. In this verse Paul refutes the argument of the Judaizers. They said that those in Antioch who led Jewish Christians to break their dietary laws by eating with Gentiles as an expression of their Christian freedom were really making Christ the cause of their sin.

Paul rejected this reasoning because it defined sin as the act of breaking the law. Paul saw sin as a deeper attitude of pride and self-sufficiency in denial of God's grace, as was the case with Adam and Eve who tried to set themselves up as equal to God. Thus Jews were already sinners in need of grace before either the giving of the law or the coming of Christ.

Verse 18. Paul's previous preaching and the agreements reached by church leaders at the Council of Jerusalem (Acts 15:1-21; Galatians 2:1-10) had removed the requirement that Gentiles be circumcised and required to observe the law. To reimpose these regulations would be to reject Christ, thus sinning against God.

Verse 19. The law, in making all who attempt to live up to it aware of their shortcomings, destroys our trust in it as a way to salvation. Hence the law helps us to die to the law, that is, no longer to believe in our ability to be good in our own strength, and thus frees us to live to God.

Verse 20. This new life in God has three dimensions: (1) It comes through Jesus Christ's death and resurrection (Romans 6:5). In dying with Christ, we say no to our old self; and in rising with Christ, we say yes to a new life of gratitude and responsibility. We no longer live to ourselves, but Christ lives in and through us (Galatians 4:19). (2) This new life is still lived in the flesh (the world). There is no miraculous escape from the drudgery, ambiguity, and pain of everyday life. We live now in faith, however; that is, we see life from a new perspective, that of Christ's forgiving love and call to service and witness. (3) The object of this new outlook is "the Son of God, who loved me and gave himself for me" (John 3:16). When it really hits me that the Son of God subjected himself to death out of love for me, my whole approach to life is radically changed. What else can I do but offer my all to Christ?

> Were the whole realm of nature mine,
> that were an offering far too small;
> love so amazing, so divine,
> demands my soul, my life, my all.[2]

This is a far greater demand than just keeping the law; but it is undertaken from a much different motivation—not from the desire to justify ourselves, but with the gratitude for an unspeakable gift.

Verse 21. This verse summarizes the previous argument. To require the Gentiles to become Jews in order to be Christian (verse 14) would reinstate the law (verse 18). This would deny God's grace and destroy the effect of Christ's sacrifice on the cross. The power of the law is removed when Christians die to the old (verse 19) and rise to the new (verse 20). Law (human effort) and grace (God's love) are mutually exclusive; we must choose to trust in one or the other.

INTRODUCE OUR NEED

May 1 is celebrated as Labor Day in many parts of the world, although not in the United States. The origin of this observance and the reason for its not being recognized in the US are directly related to the theme of this session—"Delivered From Bondage."

Labor Day is widely observed on May 1 because the "Eight-hour Day Movement" began in Chicago on May Day, 1867. Over ten thousand workers at the McCormick Reaper Plant left their jobs and marched through the streets in what a newspaper called "the largest procession ever seen on the streets of Chicago." As a result, some factories gave their employees the eight-hour day; but most did not. Strikes and agitation continued year after year as workers sought a greater measure of freedom from the unremitting toil and harsh working conditions of their factory jobs. There was no grace in the attitudes of most factory owners, who brought in strikebreakers to put down the strikes. Finally, in 1884, seventeen years later, the predecessor of the American Federation of Labor passed a resolution that read, "Resolved . . . that eight hours shall constitute a legal day's labor from and after May 1, 1886." Then, on that day, 340,000 workers in 12,000 factories across the country laid down their tools. Over 80,000 of these workers were in Chicago, nearly all of whom marched up Michigan Avenue, singing arm-in-arm.

The demonstrations continued on May 2 and 3; and on the evening of May 4, 3000 workers gathered near Haymarket Square for another rally, for which the mayor had issued a permit. After protest talks by a newspaper editor and a labor leader and while a Methodist lay preacher named Samuel Fielden was speaking, a formation of 180 armed police attacked the crowd, which by then had dwindled to 200. Suddenly, a dynamite bomb went off in the middle of the police, killing one and injuring many others. To this day no one knows who threw it. The frightened police reacted by firing wildly into the crowd, killing at least four workers and wounding more than twenty others. In the panic, the police actually killed seven of their own men. In the outcry that followed, freedom of speech and assembly were suspended in Chicago and other cities around the country. Homes were searched and ransacked without warrants, hundreds of labor and ethnic community leaders were arrested, and suspects were beaten and tortured. The press stirred up the public to turn against labor unions, and everyone cried for "law and order."

Eight men were eventually brought to trial, of whom one died a mysterious death in prison; four were hanged; and three, including Samuel Fielden, were later pardoned by Governor John Peter Altgeld. It is now generally recognized that most if not all of these eight were innocent of any crime; they were simply victims of a purge to get rid of labor leaders.

This series of events, known thereafter as "The Haymarket Affair," gave great impetus to the struggle of laboring people around the world for greater freedom, fairer wages, and better working conditions. Although the issues that led to Haymarket are still with us today, people in the US have moved the Labor Day observance to September in order not to be reminded of that day.

The early leadership of the labor union movement participated from a variety of motives, of course; but many, like Samuel Fielden, were moved by a deeply religious concern for the liberty and well-being of ordinary working people. The laws of the day severely limited the freedom of such people. Fielden and others placed human rights above property rights and knew that persons were "justified not by the works of the law but through faith in Jesus Christ" (Galatians 2:16).

Samuel Fielden had a deep sense of the full measure of human freedom under God. His faith led him courageously to defy unjust laws in order to bring the grace of God into the lives of working people in the concrete form of the eight-hour day—something we now take for granted. So it is appropriate that we introduce the biblical theme "Delivered From Bondage"—usually thought of in terms of Gentile freedom from bondage to the Jewish law—by telling the story of the Haymarket Eight, who made such sacrifices to obtain the freedom of workers from unjust laws.

LESSON PLAN

Begin by asking the class members to give their definitions of freedom. Introduce your own or a dictionary definition. One source puts it this way: "Freedom is release from outside control. It is the liberty to live one's own life. In the Old Testament freedom is understood specifically as freedom from slavery. In the New Testament freedom is the new relationship to God that Christ gives to . . . [humans]. In Christ . . . [human beings are] set free from bondage to sin and death. In the teaching of the church . . . [human] freedom may be used to oppose God. . . . However, God's power is . . . that which makes . . . [us] truly free."[3]

Next, ask the class members to list the freedoms for which they are thankful. Include both "freedoms *from* . . ." and "freedoms **of** or **for**. . . ." Class members might mention freedom *from* hunger, want, fear, sin, oppression, war, tyranny, violence, slavery, and bondage to the law. Gratitude might be expressed for freedom *of* or *for* worship, speech, assembly, expression, safety, food, clothing, shelter, vocation, love, service, support, and justice. Regarding these freedoms, ask: *How were these freedoms secured for us? How are they preserved today? To whom are they guaranteed and to whom denied? How might laws either protect or deprive some persons of these freedoms? Which freedoms are provided by Christ and which by human efforts? How might the two be in conflict with each other? How might freedom in Christ motivate us to express concern for the denial of freedom to others?*

Tell the story of Samuel Fielden and "The Haymarket Affair." Then ask the class members for their comments on the relationship between Christian freedom and political and economic freedoms.

Next, drawing on the commentary above and the material in the student book [pages 5–11], lead the class members in discussion using the questions below. If you prefer to lecture, you may wish to use the questions as the basis for your presentation.

(1) *Why do you think some early Christian leaders advocated adherence to the law? Why do we hold on to old ideas?*

The reasons some early Jewish Christians and we cling to old ways of thinking and acting might include: the desire for stability, a sense that things are working well as they are, the pull of habit, the fear of the new and different, laziness, reluctance to examine new ideas, comfort with the familiar, fear of loss of status or privilege, the influence of propaganda, and/or obedience to established authority.

Ask the class members for examples of new ideas they have had a hard time accepting, such as a new hymnal, a new Bible translation, new ways of worship, the ordination of women, and so forth. How do we decide on the substance of new proposals? How do we evaluate our own feelings about change? Compare the reluctance to accept the idea of freedom from the laws of Judaism in the first century to opposition to the eight-hour day in the nineteenth century, both in terms of the above causes of resistance and the deliverance from bondage by the gospel of Christ.

(2) *"In what ways does the church of today try to set rules? How do these rules help or hinder your life of faith?"* [student book, page 9].

The student book raises these questions in relation to the Jerusalem Council (Acts 15:1-21; Galatians 2:1-10), in which a compromise was reached on rules for Gentile Christians. Think of regulations in your church, spoken and unspoken, governing use of the kitchen, dress for church attendance, pastoral visitation, the conduct of committee meetings, budgets and spending, how decisions get made, how conflicts are resolved, and how pastoral changes are handled. Ask: *Who ensures that these rules are kept? Are any of these rules perceived as bondage? If so, by whom? How do persons respond who feel imprisoned by them? What happens if the rules are broken? How is grace offered and received? How is freedom in Christ experienced in our congregation?*

(3) *"What are some other components of the freedom that comes from justification by grace?"* [student book, page 11].

The student book lists freedom from bondage to sin, religious coercion, government tyranny, and human differences. It stresses the challenge to live righteously as a more important result of freedom than the overcoming of constraints to personal liberty. At this point in the session emphasize the close link between freedom and responsibility. We cannot have one without the other. Paul did not just revel in his own freedom in Christ; he risked his life to ensure it for the Galatians and others.

Samuel Fielden and the early labor leaders opposed the power of factory owners and police to bring the freedoms of decent livelihood and fair working conditions to exploited immigrant workers. Ask: *How can we use our freedoms in responsible ways and extend them to others?*

Close the session by having the class members sing "When I Survey the Wondrous Cross" or "The Voice of God Is Calling." Then ask class members to pray in unison the prayer printed at the end of the chapter in the student book.

[1] From *Abingdon Bible Handbook,* by Edward P. Blair (Abingdon Press, 1975); page 277.

[2] From "When I Survey the Wondrous Cross," in *The United Methodist Hymnal* (Copyright © 1989 by The United Methodist Publishing House); 298. Used by permission.

[3] From *Christian Word Book,* by J. Sherrell Hendricks (Graded Press, 1968); page 120.

TRY ANOTHER METHOD

Focus on the Council of Jerusalem, which dealt with the issue of law and grace relative to Gentile converts, and on a present-day issue of comparable importance for your group—for example, one of the issues mentioned above or some other issue, such as procedures for budgets and spending or the form used for taking Communion. Assign half the class members to the ancient issue, the rest to the modern one.

Have one group read Acts 15:1-21 and Galatians 2:1-10. Then divide that group into two smaller groups, representing the Judaizers and the Freedom Party. Ask each group to prepare to defend their position. Likewise, have the other half of the class form two smaller groups to prepare arguments on the contemporary issue, one taking the freedom side, the other that of order and tradition. Encourage people to take a side they personally differ with in order to develop more appreciation for it.

Have both simulations presented, the ancient then the modern, with you as moderator. Instruct both groups first to present their cases and then to negotiate a compromise. For the ancient issue, compare the group's solution with the one worked out by the early church. For the modern one, evaluate the solution in light of the emphasis in this session on justification by faith alone, deliverance from bondage, and freedom in Christ.

Chapter Two

ADOPTED AS GOD'S CHILDREN

PURPOSE

To help us realize that adoption into God's family makes us all equally children of God

BIBLE PASSAGE

Galatians 3:1-5, 23–4:7
Background: Galatians 3:1–4:7

> ### CORE VERSE
> God sent his Son ... to redeem those who were under the law, so that we might receive adoption as children. (Galatians 4:4-5)

GET READY

As you begin preparation, pray for God's presence in your midst, guiding you and your class members as you study God's Word together.

If possible, read the verses for this session in several translations. Also read one or more commentaries on the passage and articles on the New Testament understanding of "Adoption" in some Bible word books.

Think through your own responses to the five questions in the student book. If you plan to use the activity suggested in "Try Another Method," have magazine pictures on hand for the exercise on inclusiveness.

BIBLE BACKGROUND

This part of Paul's letter contains his appeal to the Galatians, based on experience and Scripture, to hold firm to their liberty in Christ.

Galatians 3:1. The chapter begins with an emotional appeal to the Galatians, whom Paul called "foolish" ("dear idiots,"[1] "slow thinking,"[2] "stupid"[3]). "Who has bewitched you?" ("been casting a spell,"[4] "put a spell on,"[5] "hoodwinked"[6]), Paul asked. In Paul's view no one would willingly leave the faith, so someone must have been exerting undue influence on them. That Jesus died on the cross to save sinners is a central teaching of the Christian faith. How could the Galatians deny it or let the Judaizers convince them otherwise?

Verse 2. Paul pointed to his readers' experience of being filled with the Spirit and asked whether that came from doing or from believing. The blessing of the Holy Spirit brings joy, revelation, an intimate relationship, partnership, assurance, and confidence about the future (Romans 8:15-17, 28, 37; 1 Corinthians 12:4-11, 27-31; 2 Corinthians 1:21-22; 5:5; 1 Thessalonians 1:5-6). How could they turn their backs on all these gifts of God and move back into bondage to the law?

Verse 3. The Galatians had begun a journey in God's Spirit. How could they return to life in "the flesh," which is variously translated as "the material,"[7] "by your own power,"[8] "by human effort,"[9] and "outward observances"[10]?

Verse 4. Did the rich experience of life in the Spirit that they had mean nothing to the Galatians? How could they so easily cast all this away? The phrase "if it really was for nothing" indicates that Paul still had hopes that his appeal would have an effect and that the Galatians would see the error of their ways.

Verse 5. The implication here is that the spiritual gifts and wonders (1 Corinthians 12:10, 28-29) that had occurred among them could not have come from the law but only from their trust in the message Paul had proclaimed on his earlier visit. The point of all these rhetorical questions was that Paul's readers were foolish to throw away the spiritual riches of the gospel to practice observance of the law, as the Judaizers wanted them to do.

Verses 23-26. Prior to the advent of faith in Christ for salvation, the law served as a "disciplinarian" ("strict governess,"[11] "put in charge,"[12] "schoolmaster,"[13] "tutor"[14]) to lead us to Christ. The Greek word here is *paidagogos* (pedagogue), which was the term for the slave responsible for supervising Greek boys ages six to sixteen. He was to accompany the boy to school, carry his slate, keep him from loitering, protect his virtue, teach him manners, and use coercive discipline as needed. So the law was not a teacher of faith but simply a preparation for it. When faith came on the scene (Galatians 3:25), the law's authority ended. Hence the law was not evil or even useless. It kept us in protective custody, so to speak, so that no serious harm could come to us. But now that Christ has come, the law is needed no longer. Jesus ushered in a new era of faith, which is open to both Jews and Gentiles (Galatians 2:16, 20-21).

Verse 27. The transformation from death to life symbolized by baptism marks the entrance into this new era. From subservience to the power of law (or to "the elemental spirits of the world" [Galatians 4:3]), we have shifted our allegiance to a new Lord, Jesus Christ. Having cast off the garments of the old life, stepped into the baptismal pool for the sacramental act of cleansing, and then come forth to don the white robes of a new life, we have "clothed ourselves with Christ." The language here suggests the image of being wrapped in Christ, living in him like a new habitat that shapes all we have and are. In 2 Corinthians 5:17, Paul puts it like this: "So if anyone is in Christ, there is a new creation: everything old has passed away; see, everything has become new!" We have a new Master. We have a new identity—no longer Mary Smith, but Mary **Christian**! We have a new status—righteous in God's sight. We have a new character (described in Colossians 3:12-17). We have a new community—the church.

Verse 28. In this community there are no distinctions. In baptism all old biases and discriminations have been put to death. When we accept Christ, we also accept all whom he has redeemed as one with us because we are one in him. Labels such as Jew and Greek, slave and free, male and female, black and white, and rich and poor no longer apply. "All . . . are one in Christ Jesus." The barriers that divide people disappear in the waters of baptism. To continue to hold on to these barriers is to deny the power of the gospel to transform. As Peter put it after his vision, "God shows no partiality" (Acts 10:34).

Verse 29. When we are in Christ, we also are descendants of Abraham and Sarah, not by blood, but through a common attitude of faith in God's promise and grace (Galatians 3:7, 9, 14). God's inclusiveness puts an end to the attitudes of prejudice and superiority brought by the law.

Galatians 4:1-3. The word *heirs* provides the transition from the previous verse. The heirs of Abraham (that is, the Jews of Paul's time) were like minors who could not touch the inherited property but must follow the wishes of guardians and trustees until becoming adults.

In this respect the Jews were no different than the Gentiles, whom Paul saw as slaves or spirit worshipers. This is variously translated as "slaves of the ruling spirits of the universe,"[15] "under the authority of basic moral principles,"[16] "ruled by the deeply entrenched patterns of the culture,"[17] and "in subjection to the elementary knowledge which this world can supply."[18] That is, prior to meeting Christ, we are shaped by alien influences in which we put our faith to give meaning to our lives. But these continue to separate us from God until Christ breaks through to us. This inheritance, into which we are born, only leads us astray. We need to be rescued from bondage to it.

Verses 4-7. The "fullness of time" (verse 4) corresponds to the "date set by the father" (verse 2), the time appointed by God when the inheritance can be claimed and the child enters full adulthood. God sent the Son, born as a human and subject to human systems, to liberate us from slavery to all these systems, whether law, principle, cultural patterns, earthly knowledge, or the spirits of nature. Freed from the status of slaves to systems, we are accepted as children and heirs of God. When the Spirit of Christ fills our hearts, we are moved to cry, "Daddy," addressing God in a spirit of intimacy and love.

As mature adults in God's sight we no longer require a supervisor to guide and protect us. Nor are we controlled by the standards of culture, fashion, or secular belief. Through the redemption of Christ, the restraining walls of those households are torn down; and we are adopted into God's family of freedom and grace. This adoption is initiated by God, confers a new status as children in God's household, and offers the rich heritage of abundant life in the Spirit.

INTRODUCE OUR NEED

Gloria, a high school girl from one of the South Pacific islands, had come to Hawaii with her father, leaving her mother behind. Gloria felt isolated and lonely. She was also burdened with homework in a strange school and housework in a small apartment, where she had to care for her father and other relatives as they arrived home from work.

Stopping off after school one day to do her homework at the church where her father was custodian, her eyes fell on a Bible. She opened it and saw the words, "Come to me, all you that are weary and are carrying heavy burdens, and I will give you rest" (Matthew 11:28).

"Those words really touched my heart," Gloria told me. "A voice inside was saying, 'God knows what you're going through and wants to help you.' And so my desire really grew to know Jesus more." Jesus was speaking to her and offering her comfort and acceptance in the midst of the turmoil and drudgery of her life. A profound peace filled her heart. "This was the first time I ever felt God was real to me," she said, "when the Word became so alive." The light of Christ's love flowed into Gloria's heart, her burden was lifted, and she felt joy and hope once again.

From that point on, Gloria's life changed dramatically. Although she came from a Christian background, she had not been attending church. Now she started going to worship, Sunday school, and youth group and was the only youth in the pastor's Bible class. She said, "I was hungry to know God more. God became so real, and I didn't want to miss any worship." Gloria also found a friend in the church secretary, who provided the concern and support she had missed because of the absence of her mother.

In her developing prayer life, Gloria was led to turn her problems over to the Lord. "I said to God, 'OK, I lift my problem at home to you.' God said, 'Love others as you love yourself.' But I'd say, 'There's no way I'm going to love these relatives of mine, Lord.' But then I prayed, 'Only through the love of Christ can I love my relatives. Lord, create in me a new heart!' And you know, I don't hold grudges against my relatives any more. I look at them from a new perspective. The negative feelings are gone. I'm glad to see them come to my house now; I'm glad to help them."

A deepening prayer life, changed attitude, and regular participation in worship and Bible study gradually led Gloria to decide to join the church—a multi-ethnic congregation well-known for its inclusiveness. "Long before I went through the ceremony, I already was a member of the church of Christ," she told me. "Going through the membership training, being baptized, and standing before the congregation, though, has caused me to devote more of my life to the church. I want to reach out to inactive persons and share my faith with them."

When the time was ripe, God sent Jesus into Gloria's heart to redeem her from loneliness and slavery to her resentments, family, and culture. She was adopted as a child of God; and her heart cried, "Abba!" She was no longer a slave but a child and heir of God's promise (Galatians 4:4-7). She was baptized into Christ, clothed with new attitudes and habits, and accepted into a faith community in which "all . . . are one in Christ Jesus" (Galatians 3:28).

LESSON PLAN

Begin by recalling some of the adoption experiences shared by class members during the previous session. Then tell the family adoption story that opens the chapter in the student book and the spiritual adoption story of Gloria above. Observe that the sense of belonging to family comes more from genuine acceptance than from blood ties. I feel closer to and have more in common with some fellow Christians than with some of my blood relatives. This may be true of some of your class members as well. The deep sense of belonging in the family of faith comes from the assurance that we all belong to Christ—regardless of gender, language, nationality, race, denomination, or doctrinal viewpoint.

Next, drawing on the commentary above and the material in the student book [pages 12–20], lead the class members in discussion using the questions below. If you prefer to lecture, you may wish to use the questions as the basis for your presentation.

(1) *"What role, if any, has strict discipline played in your life?"* [student book, page 16].

This question grows out of the discussion of Galatians 3:23-26 [student book, pages 15–16], in which Paul referred to the law as a disciplinarian that prepared people for the coming of Christ. The class members might come up with examples from sports, studies, music, resisting temptation, risking danger, preparing for a test, body building, or devotional life to illustrate the need for discipline. Ask about each: *How did you feel when you were under this discipline? What effort did it require? What help did you need to maintain it? What happened when you broke it? What was the goal toward which you were striving? Did you reach it? When and why did you cease the strict discipline? What do we need in our lives to balance discipline? What does Paul's message to the Galatians offer in this regard?*

(2) *"We have freedom as adopted children of God, yet we are called to live moral lives. How do you deal with the tension between spiritual freedom and moral responsibility?"* [student book, page 16].

This question raises the issue of freedom and responsibility. The gospel liberates us from the legal requirements of salvation but challenges us to deny ourselves, take up our cross, and follow Jesus. Some observers of American culture note that persons in the generation shaped by the Great Depression and World War II tended to live by the ethic of self-denial, while the postwar generation sought self-fulfillment. Is the abundant life found through limiting our desires for the sake of higher good, or is it found through activities that encourage self-expression and build self-esteem?

Paul was telling the Galatians that as God's children they were free from bondage to the law, accepted as they were into God's family, and thus free to live out of a motivation of gratitude and love. The key here is being "clothed with Christ" through baptism. We cannot be enveloped in the love of Christ and at the same time live like the devil. The Spirit of Christ is our guide for everyday living. Like Jesus, we are called to live a life of caring love, self-giving service, and commitment to the reign of God. We do this, not out of a sense of duty or fear, but in heartfelt gratitude for God's saving grace.

Ask: *Are you motivated more by self-denial or by self-fulfillment? What would characterize the lifestyle of persons "clothed with Christ"?*

(3) *"Why have we resisted the clear meaning of Galatians 3:27-28 for so long?"* [student book, page 17].

The clear meaning is that all are equal, all are accepted, all are one in Christ Jesus—regardless of race, gender, or economic status. The expressions of resistance in attitude, behavior, and social structure are referred to as racism, sexism, and classism. They are rooted in our desires for self-preservation and self-advancement, our needs for power and control, our

fear of intimacy and failure, our hungers for possessions and comforts, our senses of insecurity and inadequacy—in other words, the self-centeredness we call sin.

Invite class members to share experiences in which they have either encountered prejudice and rejection or expressed these attitudes themselves. Ask: *Is our church all-inclusive? What kinds of persons do we consciously or unconsciously turn away? What are the reasons for this? How can we become more accepting? How can we better exhibit in our congregation the truth that "all . . . are one in Christ Jesus"?*

(4) *"What does it mean to you to know that you are a member of God's family?"* [student book, page 18].

The student book emphasizes that adoption into God's family makes us all equal in value. All of us are needed to fulfill the ministry of Christ's church. The question then becomes, "How close a tie do we feel to the church in all its diversity, and how committed are we to offer our gifts and energies to its ministry?" Remind the class members of the tensions between Jew and Gentile in the Roman house churches and of the controversy between the Judaizers and the freedom party in the churches of Galatia that Paul was trying to resolve.

Ask: *Are there any issues or events that have caused disagreement in our congregation? If so, what caused the dispute? How was it handled? Where does it stand now? What are the obstacles to greater unity and harmony? What can we do to strengthen the sense of belonging in our congregation? How does Paul's idea of adoption as children of God speak to this need?*

Suggestions for deepening the unity of a congregation include: praying for healing and acceptance; holding meetings to encourage free expression of complaints, appreciations, and offers to help; calling on inactive members and listening to their concerns and needs; praying for individual joys and concerns in morning worship; making intentional efforts to invite newcomers in the neighborhood to attend church, regardless of race or class; assigning older members to newcomers as hosts or sponsors; and starting focused small groups for persons with particular interests or needs.

(5) *"How do you feel about being a fellow worker with God?"* [student book, page 20].

The student book section entitled "No Longer a Slave but a Child" notes the differences that Christ makes in our lives: We relate to God with affection instead of dread; we become partners rather than soldiers under orders; and our reconciliation replaces our separation.

In responding to this question, some class members may express preference for a more distant, respectful, and awe-filled attitude toward the Creator. Others may feel a more intimate relationship with "Abba." Welcome an exchange of views on this issue, and explain that both approaches are biblical and appropriate. What is so remarkable is that through Christ, the all-powerful, all-knowing, and ever-present God has become open to a relationship of love and intimacy with sinful human beings like us. Moreover this God needs us in the ongoing process of creation—making a better world. Remind the class members of the heritage of God's love, grace, and eternal life that we have as heirs of God. Stress that it is in response to these gifts that we dedicate ourselves to live as true children of God.

Depending on the emphasis with which you wish to end the session, close by singing "In Christ There Is No East or West," "Many Gifts, One Spirit," or "O Jesus, I Have Promised." Pray in unison the prayer that ends the chapter in the student book.

[1] From *The New Testament in Modern English,* revised edition, by J.B. Phillips. © J.B. Phillips, 1958, 1960, 1972. Used by permission of Macmillan Publishing Co., Inc.

[2] From *The Cotton Patch Version of Paul's Epistles,* by Clarence Jordan (Association Press, 1968).

[3] From *The New English Bible.* © The delegates of the Oxford University Press and the Syndics of the Cambridge University Press 1961, 1970. Reprinted by permission.

[4] From *The New Testament in Modern English,* revised edition.

[5] From *The Bible in Today's English Version* (American Bible Society, 1966, 1971, 1976).

[6] From *The Cotton Patch Version of Paul's Epistles.*

[7] From *The New English Bible.*

[8] From *The Bible in Today's English Version.*

[9] From *The New International Version,* Copyright © 1973, 1978, 1984 International Bible Society. Used by permission of Zondervan Publishing Company.

[10] From *The New Testament in Modern English,* revised edition.

[11] From *The New Testament in Modern English,* revised edition.

[12] From *The New International Version.*

[13] From the King James Version of the Bible.

[14] From *The New English Bible.*

[15] From *The Bible in Today's English Version.*

[16] From *The New Testament in Modern English,* revised edition.

[17] From *The Cotton Patch Version of Paul's Epistles.*

[18] From *The Letters to the Galatians and Ephesians,* by William Barclay (The Westminster Press, 1958).

TRY ANOTHER METHOD

For Question 1, ask the class members to decide on a spiritual discipline—such as praying daily for one another, reading a chapter in the Bible every day, or fasting one meal a week and giving the savings to a hunger project—to which they will all commit themselves for the remaining three weeks of this study.

For Question 3, pass around pictures clipped from magazines of persons of various races, classes, nationalities, and lifestyles; then ask about each: *What gifts does this person bring to the human community? Would this person be welcome in our church? Who is there like this person in our vicinity to whom we might reach out in Christian love?*

For Question 4, draw a horizontal line on a chalkboard or large piece of paper and place numbers from 1 (distant) to 10 (very close) along it. Ask members to write their names at a point on the line indicating the strength of their sense of belonging to the family of faith. (An alternative is to draw the line on the floor and have the members stand along it.) Then ask all the class members to share why they placed themselves where they did, what factors contributed to their feeling of distance or closeness, and what can be done to bind them and others closer to one another in Christ.

FREED TO GROW

PURPOSE

To help us explore the tension in our spiritual journeys between growing in grace and turning back

BIBLE PASSAGE

Galatians 4:8-20
Background: Galatians 4:8-31

CORE VERSE

Now, however, that you have come to know God, or rather to be known by God, how can you turn back again to the weak and beggarly elemental spirits? How can you want to be enslaved to them again?
(Galatians 4:9)

GET READY

This session provides an opportunity for you and the other members of your class to evaluate your spiritual well-being in terms of worship and devotional practices, attitudes, habits, loyalties, and friendships that either foster or obstruct spiritual health and growth. Prayerfully consider using the activity suggested in "Try Another Method" below, for which you will need to prepare a questionnaire.

Read the Bible Passage and consult commentaries on the passage.

Arrange to have copies of the Sunday worship service bulletin in the session for members to look at.

BIBLE BACKGROUND

In our Bible Passage, Paul first urges the Galatians not to reject the relationship they have had with God and then refers to the pain their backsliding is causing him, their friend and teacher.

Galatians 4:8-9. Paul deplored the fact that his Galatian friends were being tempted back into bondage to either the law or pagan deities. The phrase "elemental spirits" (verse 9) can also be translated "elementary things" or "principles," which suggests that Paul was comparing the Jewish Christians' former subservience to the law to the Gentile Christians' former idol worship. Whether these persons were enslaved to beings and spirits or to rules and principles of conduct, the result was the same: They were prevented from knowing the one true God. Now that they had come to know God through Jesus, Paul could not see why they would want to give that up.

The elementary stage in religion, whether legalistic or idolatrous, is weak and poverty-stricken—weak because it has no power to save from sin and poverty-stricken in the light of God's wondrous grace. A personal relationship with God, in which we know and are known by the One whom we can call Daddy, is in a different realm from the Galatians' previous religious experience. They had moved from the cellar to the penthouse and now wanted to go back. Incredible!

Verse 10. Every religion has its special times and seasons. Whether the Galatians had come out of Judaism or out of worship of the Greco-Roman gods and goddesses, they knew about holy days and festivals. Christians have them too, but the problem with holy days and festivals in any religion is that they separate sacred from secular. We are led to believe that if we go to church on Sunday and pay special attention to the Christmas and Easter seasons, we are somehow pleasing God. Yet the difference between religion and faith that Paul was pointing to is that we are called to give *all* our time and life to God, not just the sacred seasons. Our relationship with God is not just something we observe at certain times, it is a life commitment.

Verse 11. If the Galatians turned back—having once said no to the old and yes to the new in baptism—Paul's missionary labor would be made null and void. All the trials he had endured, all the effort he had made to nurture them, all his agonizing prayer and concern, would be lost. No wonder Paul was upset. He had invested a lot in the Galatian Christians. He was going all out to stop their backsliding.

Verse 12. Paul made a personal appeal to the Galatians' friendship. He had argued from Scripture, doctrine, and experience. Then, because of their previous friendship, he begged them to give up the supposed benefits of the teaching that was attracting them and to return to abide with him in Christ. Paul wanted them to follow his example in staying with the move from slavery to freedom. They had not hurt him up to this point; in fact, they had treated him with utmost kindness and hospitality during his visit. If they turned their backs on the gospel he had taught them, however, they would hurt him deeply.

Verses 13-14. Apparently, the Galatian Christians had cared for Paul through an illness or infirmity. Some think, because of the mention in Galatians 4:15 of their willingness to give him their eyes, that Paul had an eye ailment—possibly resulting from his having been blinded on the Damascus Road. This may or may not be the same affliction he referred to in 2 Corinthians 12:7 as "a thorn . . . in the flesh." In addition to an eye disease, this ailment has variously been identified as malaria, stammering, violent headaches, epilepsy, the persecutions Paul suffered, and his less than imposing physical appearance (2 Corinthians 10:10). Many ancient and Reformation church fathers believed the affliction to have been a spiritual problem—Satan's temptations of the flesh from which Paul was unable to gain release (1 Corinthians 9:26-27; 10:12-13; 2 Corinthians 2:11).

Whatever it was, Paul thanked the Galatians for accepting him in this condition, however repulsive it may have been. The phrase "you did not scorn or despise me" could be translated "you did not turn from me with loathing" or "you did not spit on me." This was the way people in that day treated epileptics so as to shield themselves from the evil spirit by which they thought epileptics were possessed. Instead, the Galatians had received Paul like an angel (manifestation of God) or like Jesus himself, which reminds us of Jesus blessing those who served the needy: "As you did it to one of the least of these who are members of my family, you did it to me" (Matthew 25:40).

Verse 15. How could the Galatians so soon have lost the sense of joy, love, and well-being that had come from their initial experience of salvation? They had been willing to sacrifice their very eyes in order to restore Paul to health; and now, due to the harmful influence of those who had come to them during Paul's absence, they were ready to cast that all away and turn back to their old life. This was a clear case of backsliding. Like Esau, they had sold their birthright for a mess of pottage.

Verse 16. Paul was laying it on the line, and his rebuke was hard to take. It is natural to view one speaking so bluntly as an enemy. The truth hurts. No one likes a person who speaks the hard but necessary word. Yet Paul wondered, given their former love for him, why their attitude had changed so quickly. One should be able to speak frankly to friends. He had been "speaking the truth in love" (Ephesians 4:15), but they had rejected him for it.

Verse 17. The "they" here refers to Paul's opponents, who had been courting and enticing the Galatians (Galatians 3:1) with seductive words and false promises. "They" were trying to cut them off from the influence of Paul and the gospel in order to win them back to the old ways. The luring of Christians into Judaism would bring much glory and credit to the Judaizers. Just as Paul's missionary motives had been criticized by his opponents (Galatians 1:10), so now Paul was questioning theirs. These persons did not have the best interests of the Galatians at heart, he argued. Rather, they were seeking to manipulate people back into bondage to the law and thereby to gain recognition from those who had sent them on this mission (just as Paul had done in his persecution of Christians before his conversion; see Acts 9:1-2).

Verse 18. It is fine to be praised when one has done a good thing, whether by Paul or by some other persons. Our actions must be judged by the purity and merit of the end we seek, however. Paul's heart ached for his Galatian friends. He had put so much into winning them and did not want to lose them. This is the "good purpose" of which he spoke.

Verse 19. Paul's love for the Galatians was like that of a mother who goes through the pain of childbirth—not once, but twice—to bring new life into the world.

He had labored once to win them to Christ on his missionary journey. Now, in the deep agony of prayer and persuasion, he was doing so again. The phrase "until Christ is formed in you" is a marvelous way of speaking about the development of Christian character and commitment. It is like the oak tree growing from the acorn or the butterfly emerging from the cocoon. The seed had been planted; the word had been preached; the initial "yes" had been spoken. The long nurturing process had not yet come to fruition, however. In fact, it had been obstructed by Paul's opponents. The formation process had come to a premature halt. The child that was born had had its growth stunted. Paul, the loving parent, was again urging the Galatians to grow up in Christ and to take on the form to which God was calling them. Paul's lament here is similar to that which God expressed through Hosea about the wayward children of Israel:

> When Israel was a child, I loved him,
>   and out of Egypt I called my son.
> The more I called them,
>   the more they went from me;
> they kept sacrificing to the Baals,
>   and offering incense to idols.
> Yet it was I who taught Ephraim to walk,
>   I took them up in my arms;
>   but they did not know that I healed them.
> I led them with cords of human kindness,
>   with bands of love.
>
> (Hosea 11:1-4)

Verse 20. Here Paul seems to be catching himself in a contradiction—and halfway apologizing for it. His motive was concern for the well-being of his readers, but he had been writing in tones of anger and rebuke. As is often the case, if he could speak with them face to face, he would have modified his approach and been more conciliatory. "I am perplexed about you" could also be translated "I am worried about you, at a loss about you, or don't know how to deal with you." Paul was frustrated and grieving because those he loved so much appeared to be slipping from his grasp and turning their backs on God's abundant grace.

INTRODUCE OUR NEED

When I met him, Cecil had just retired from the Navy and, at age thirty-nine, was preparing for a career in real estate. His faith journey had begun when he was seven. At that time he was baptized by immersion in an African-American Baptist church. "I felt like somebody special that day," he told me. "I wore white, and after the baptism I changed my clothes and had a different place to sit in the church. This was the most memorable experience of my life."

Cecil was raised in the faith by his grandmother. "We went to church and Sunday school and stayed all day. Grandmother was the mother of the church; it was so much a part of her life. I saw through her faith what faith could do. She was a living example." He remembers his mother and grandmother saying grace at meals and praying before bed at night. "My mother would sing spirituals while doing the laundry, with tears in her eyes. This memory is deep and abiding."

When Cecil went off to the Navy at age eighteen, his grandmother gave him a Bible and told him always to pray and go to church. "My grandmother asked me to keep God with me. She told me to read my Bible and said that I would find comfort in it. I did get lonely, and I read my Bible often. I made it a point to go to church even though the people I was with did not. I experienced individual prayer and meditation. If anybody was on my side, God was." The example and guidance of his mother and grandmother and the churchgoing habits they had instilled in him kept Cecil related to the church and in touch with God even when external circumstances pulled him away.

There were many temptations, and Cecil did not always remain faithful. "Some people in the service were not from a religious environment. This caused me to begin questioning. Sometimes I was not a strong Christian. I did go carousing with the fellows." He also faced several crises that tested his faith. These included a serious illness, a court battle for custody of his children, and the command to fire a missile from his submarine. Through all this the prayers, advice, and example of his grandmother stayed with him, however; and he kept coming back to his Christian faith.

Cecil was like the Galatians—converted to Christ but tempted to turn back to other ways. Yet the foundation laid by his grandmother and her prayers for him called him back to his faith and kept him steady in the face of temptations and crises. His mother and grandmother had birthed him into the faith. He had taken on the form of Christ in baptism. While in the service he could have lost all this due to the negative influences around him. But the memory and prayers of his grandmother—like the urgings of Paul to the Galatians—brought him back to the faith.

Cecil's story has a happy ending. Today, he is an

active Christian, leading layperson, and youth Sunday school teacher. Unfortunately, we do not know whether the Galatians responded this positively to Paul's loving appeal.

LESSON PLAN

Begin by explaining that our Bible Passage from Galatians describes Paul's appeal to his readers to examine their spiritual lives. They had been converted under his ministry but in his absence had encountered corrupting influences and were tempted to turn back to their old religious practices, whether paganism or Judaism. Paul urged them, on the basis of Scripture, Christian teaching, and their experience of grace, to assess their spiritual condition and to return to faith in Christ.

We too can be tempted to turn back from our original joy and enthusiasm. Like the Galatians, we need to evaluate our spiritual well-being and to allow God's Spirit to woo us back to our original commitment. Tell the story of Cecil as one who was tempted to fall away but who was held steady in his faith by the influence and prayers of his grandmother.

Then, drawing on the commentary above and the material in the student book [pages 21–29], lead the class members in discussion using the questions below. If you prefer to lecture, you may wish to use the questions as the basis for your presentation.

(1) *"Have you ever been disappointed at how a friendship turned out? If so, what were the circumstances?"* [student book, page 24].

These questions refer to Paul's disappointment at the news that his Galatian friends had been turning back from the commitment to Christ that they made when he was with them. Ask the class members to think of friendships they have had that have turned sour and to share the reasons this happened. A friend may have broken a promise; interests may have changed; career paths may have put people in different circles; disagreements may have cooled affections; former friends may be separated by distance; or one friend may have dropped out of church activities, while the other remained active.

Then ask how persons feel about these changes. Such feelings as disappointment, resentment, relief, frustration, hostility, grief, regret, alienation, and rejection may be mentioned. Comment that similar feelings must have been in Paul's heart as he wrote this letter, which explains the tone of his plea. Also observe

that our relationships are all interrelated; when a friendship has been disrupted, our relationships with others and with God and our feeling about ourselves can also be affected. This is why the quality of our relationships is one indicator of our overall spiritual health.

(2) *"What practices, if any, do you know of that seem like those to which Paul objected?"* [student book, page 25].

The Galatian Christians, both Jew and Gentile, were being tempted to fall back into their former religious practices—observance of special days, rites, and rules. This was damaging their faith and their spiritual health.

Ask the class members if there are worship practices in your congregation or in their devotional lives that are hurtful to their spiritual growth. Distribute copies of the Sunday worship service bulletin so the class members can review your order of worship and comment on individual items. For example, worship might be characterized by draggy or unfamiliar hymns, too many (or too few) changes, inappropriate music, lack of congregational participation, poorly planned services, too much (or too little) ritual, long or dry sermons (or even too brief sermons), visitors feeling unwelcome, a sanctuary in need of redecorating, too much chatter during the prelude, or absence of a sense of community.

Problems in personal devotional life might include lack of a daily discipline; lack of meaningful devotional resources; feeling that God is distant or that prayers are not being answered; the rigid expectations we may place on ourselves; too much dependence on having an emotional experience when we pray; difficulty in understanding the Bible; or an inadequate view of God, either seeing God as a cosmic Santa Claus to whom we tell our wants or as an impersonal Creator who is too busy for us and our needs.

Discuss what might be done to remove these obstacles to spiritual health and growth.

(3) *"What other ways of turning back from full spirituality can you name?"* [student book, page 28].

The student book mentions the following ways of backsliding in our spiritual lives; losing meaningful, spiritual worship; turning back from the truth that we are all equal in grace; repressing new ideas; judging rather than encouraging persons; and living immoral, impure, or undisciplined lives. Discuss each of these ways, asking whether slippage in any area may be affecting our growth in faith or our religious vitality.

Then ask the question printed above, raising the following possibilities, if necessary, to "prime the pump": being too self-centered in our concerns; lacking a vision for what God is calling us to become; being preoccupied with the seven last words of the church: "We have always done it this way"; believing that the church is here to meet our needs rather than those of the world; being in a rut; being so open to diversity and change that we lack direction and stability; and having a God that is "too small," along the lines described by J. B. Phillips in the chapter in the student book [pages 22–23].

(4) *At what times are you tempted to turn back?*

In commenting on the Galatians' tendency to backslide during Paul's absence, the student book suggests that we may be inclined to turn back at the change points of life, when commitment wanes, or when competing loyalties arise. Ask class members how they have dealt with these situations. Also ask about other circumstances that can pull people backward. These might include departure of a beloved pastor or friend, doubts raised by the claims of persons of another denomination or faith, death of a loved one, advent of an incurable illness, and fatigue or burnout from carrying too many duties without adequate resources or support.

Close the session with a time of prayer in which class members are invited to ask God for whatever help they need, as individuals and as a congregation, to nurture and deepen all facets of their spiritual lives. End this prayer time by having the class members sing "Take Time to Be Holy."

TRY ANOTHER METHOD

Prepare a brief questionnaire to distribute to class members, asking them to assess their own and the congregation's spiritual health on a scale of 1 (feeble), 2 (poor), 3 (so-so), 4 (coming along), 5 (stable), and 6 (robust) in each of the following areas:

(A) my personal prayer life
(B) our worship life in the congregation
(C) the quality of my friendships
(D) relationships in our congregation
(E) my attitude toward persons different from me
(F) our treatment, as a congregation, of persons different from us
(G) my ability to accept persons and ideas that I disagree with
(H) our ability as a congregation to accept persons and ideas that we disagree with
(I) the level of my commitment to Christ in the face of competing loyalties
(J) the level of our commitment as a congregation in the face of competing demands for our time and energy

As the class members complete the questionnaire, ask them to write responses to these questions:

(1) *What is blocking my (or our) spiritual growth in each of these areas?*
(2) *What might God be saying to me through this exercise about what I (or we as a congregation) need to be doing?*
(3) *What am I ready to commit myself to in each of these areas?*

Then go through the questionnaire one item at a time, inviting class members to share their ratings and their answers to the three questions, writing the answers on a chalkboard or on a large piece of paper in three columns. Pause periodically to allow interaction around people's responses, but do not force anyone to share or to comment on the responses of others.

In light of what have emerged as (1) obstacles, (2) leadings of God, and (3) commitments, develop a covenant of individual and group spiritual discipline to which persons are willing to be held accountable. Allow freedom for members not ready to make this commitment to opt out if they wish. Decide how this accountability will be maintained—in terms of devoting time in class sessions for members to share how they are doing, having extra meetings for this purpose, or regularly using this or a similar questionnaire for reflection and response.

Chapter Four

ENABLED TO BEAR FRUIT

PURPOSE

To help us express the joy of Christian freedom in the fruits of the Spirit

BIBLE PASSAGE

Galatians 5:1, 13-26
Background: Galatians 5

> ### CORE VERSES
> The fruit of the Spirit is love, joy, peace, patience, kindness, generosity, faithfulness, gentleness, and self-control. (Galatians 5:22-23)

GET READY

Read the Bible Passage, the chapter in the student book, commentaries, and the paragraphs below. Then pray for your class members.

Next, on a blank piece of paper jot down the key words in this chapter. Among those you might list are: *freedom, yoke, slave, love, Spirit, flesh, impurity, idolatry, anger, sorcery, enmity, carousing, fruit, joy, patience, peace, passion, self-control, faithfulness, generosity, competition, envy.* Then opposite each word write a word, phrase, image, or experience that it calls to mind. Examples: *impurity*—poison; *sorcery*—manipulation; *idolatry*—false gods; *competition*—beating others; *fruit*—results. Have writing materials on hand so class members can also do this exercise during the session.

BIBLE BACKGROUND

Galatians 5 opens with a reference to Galatians 4:12-31, in which Paul points to Hagar and Sarah, two women who had children by Abraham, as symbols of slavery to and freedom from the law. Children of the former, like Ishmael, are born into bondage to the flesh (law, sin, self-centeredness, desire); while those of the latter, like Isaac, are children of promise (hope, faith, grace, freedom). (Note: This is an allegorical reference only [Galatians 4:24], and it is contrary to the biblical emphasis on God's universal love for all peoples to draw from it any conclusions about God's attitude toward the present-day descendants of those persons.) Those who had accepted Christ had received the promise of freedom, and Paul urged them not to return to the way of legalism. If they did so, they would lose all the benefits of being in Christ and living in the freedom of love.

Paul then proceeded to develop these ideas, appealing to the good judgment of his readers and giving a warning to those who were stirring up trouble: Christian freedom does not mean living as you please but rather acting out of love for one another. Christians do not live by rules but in grateful response to God's love. With the Spirit's guidance we can overcome sinful desires and behavior and live Christlike lives, embodying spiritual virtues.

Given this summary of Galatians 5, let us examine the selected verses in more detail.

Galatians 5:1. Freedom in Christ is quite different from both the self-centered independence advocated by the Stoics of Paul's time and the individual pursuit of self-fulfillment that characterizes ours. Freedom in Christ comes only through the saving work of Christ in his crucifixion and resurrection and is confirmed by the gift of God's Spirit (Galatians 3:1-2). This freedom can be lost if we are not careful to exercise it responsibly; so Paul urged the Galatians—and us—to "stand firm" (1 Corinthians 15:1; 16:13).

If we do not stand firm, we will once again come under the yoke of slavery, a reference to the Roman practice of bringing home captives as slaves under an ox yoke. To preserve our freedom, we must choose faith in Christ and hold to it. To return to our former values and lifestyle (that is, circumcision [Galatians 5:2-3]) is to cut ourselves off from the grace and goodness of Christ. What counts is "faith working through love" (Galatians 5:6), and this is worth holding on to at all costs.

Verses 13-15. As usual in Paul's letters, the focus shifts from theology to ethics. Having made the case for salvation by faith, not works, Paul drew out the implications for everyday life. The call to faith is addressed to a community—brothers and sisters who belong to one another because they belong to Christ. Freedom in Christ is not the liberty to practice egotistical self-expression without regard to the effects on others. Rather, the liberation from bondage to rules and ordinances is a call to another kind of slavery—the subordination of selfish desires to a caring regard for the building up of the community and the growth and fulfillment of each member.

Freedom that fulfills the law requires both love and service. Love without service is sheer emotion, while service without love is empty duty. Just as Jesus summarized the whole law in the twin commandments to love God and neighbor (Matthew 22:37-40), so Paul reduced all ethical requirements of the Christian life to the law of neighbor love (Leviticus 19:18; also see Romans 13:8-10). The moral, religious, and political laws of the Jewish tradition are neither ignored nor negated. Rather, they are embraced and lived out in the inner desire and outer expression of serving love in response to God's grace in Christ.

This paragraph closes with a reminder to the church that Christian love is undermined by contention and backbiting. Honest disagreement and conflict are healthy and productive as people are open with one another and work through differences to deeper understanding and constructive solutions. Personal attacks, name calling, and conniving will hurt persons, destroy community, and consume the goodwill and trust upon which a growing church's life and mission must be based.

Verses 16-18. Flesh and Spirit, that is, self-indulgence versus loving acts and attitudes, are set in opposition to each other. Selfish desires contradict a loving spirit, and the Spirit of God overcomes our self-centered need for rigid regulations to control behavior. The battle in us between these two tendencies is real (Romans 7:14). To overcome sin, gain strength for the struggle, and be freed from moralism, we must submit to God's love, accept Christ's forgiveness, and be led by the Spirit.

Verses 19-21. From this list of the works of the flesh, we see that Paul is not referring exclusively to physical sins. All the behaviors mentioned have both a spiritual motivation and a physical expression. *Fornication* stems from the heart, as Jesus points out in Matthew 5:28. *Impurity* is measured, not by what goes in, but by what comes out (Matthew 12:35). *Licentiousness* proceeds from an inner disrespect for the dignity of persons, which results in using them for selfish ends. *Idolatry* is devoting one's energies, both physical and spiritual, to serving any goal—money and possessions, fame and recognition, achievement and position, and so forth—other than God. *Sorcery* employs a distorted understanding of the universe to manipulate spiritual powers and material things for self-serving ends.

Enmities, strife, jealousy, quarrels, dissensions, factions, and envy all represent division and alienation occasioned by the sin of focus on self and disregard for the feelings and needs of others.

Anger is a natural emotion evoked by frustration of our needs or denial of basic rights to others. As a healthy, authentic expression of our real selves that clears the air and leads to genuine dialogue and resolution of differences, it is not wrong or sinful. Ephesians 4:25-26 advises, "So then, putting away falsehood, let all of us speak the truth to our neighbors, for we are members of one another. Be angry but do not sin; do not let the sun go down on your anger." Honest expression of anger is being open with one another and can deepen relationships and build community. Only when anger is harbored as resentment and allowed to fester as bitterness, all the while preserving the outer facade of niceness and harmony, does it become sin. This is the kind of smoldering anger that Paul classified as a work of the flesh.

Drunkenness and carousing, while appearing as boorish, offensive behavior, are really expressions of the soul sickness known as low self-esteem, rooted in an earlier lack of love, acceptance, or discipline. All these self-centered attitudes and behaviors had infected the Galatian churches. Paul both warned those who exhibited such attitudes and behaviors that they were excluding themselves from the realm of God and urged them to allow God's Spirit to transform and empower them.

Verses 22-26. This life is characterized by the fruits of the Spirit, which also have both an inner and an outer dimension. *Love* is nurtured by loving relationships with God and other human beings and is communicated in concrete acts of care, support, and justice. *Joy,* like carousing, is an expression of a sense of celebration. The difference is that carousing lacks focus and is out of control, while joy is directed to God and is uplifting to others. *Peace* is both an inner sense of tranquility and an outer reconciliation and concord among persons, groups, and nations. Grounded in inner peace and acceptance of others, *patience* trusts the Spirit to guide the process rather than anxiously manipulating it to serve one's own ends. *Kindness, generosity,* and *gentleness* are unselfish attitudes of respect, tenderness, and concern for others, expressed in thoughtful, concrete acts of service and compassion. *Faithfulness* is a courageous, steadfast living out of an inner integrity grounded in trust and reliance on the goodness of God. *Self-control* is not a rigid, self-denying bondage to rules but rather a willing dedication of one's energies and gifts to the tasks of Christian discipleship.

These inner attitudes and outer acts are outgrowths of our saving relationship with Christ, through which our self-centered desires are transformed into a passion for life, hope, and justice. To live by the Spirit inwardly leads to being guided by the Spirit in our outer behavior. Our lives will show that we abide in God's love. As John put it, "Those who do not love a brother or sister whom they have seen, cannot love God whom they have not seen. . . . Those who love God must love their brothers and sisters also" (1 John 4:20-21).

In conclusion, Paul urged the Galatians not to have a conceited opinion of themselves, which would be expressed in attitudes and behavior that denied the worth of other persons. This could happen either by taking advantage through competition or by scheming to gain for oneself what belongs to another. Walking by the Spirit demands integrity and concern for the well-being of others.

INTRODUCE OUR NEED

The joy of Christian freedom and the fruits of the Spirit were seen in the incredible life of Sojourner Truth, whose original name was Isabella. Born of slave parents in 1793, she and her brother and sister were sold when she was nine—at the time her aging parents were turned loose by their owner as being too weak to work anymore.

In her fear and loneliness, Isabella prayed to God, begging for protection and asking how she was offending God to bring such tragedy upon herself. During her teens and young adulthood, she was sold to two other owners, saw the man she loved beaten to a pulp, was forced to marry a man named Thomas, and bore five children. She decided to escape, found refuge in a Quaker home, but then was persuaded by her previous owner to return. As she was climbing into his carriage, however, she had a powerful conversion experience that she describes this way:

I could feel [God] burnin', burnin', burnin', all around me, an' goin' through me. . . . An' I said, "O somebody, somebody, stand between God an' me! for it burns me!"

Then . . . I felt as if . . . an umbrella . . . came between me an' the light, an' I felt it was somebody . . . that loved me. . . . And finally somethin' spoke out in me an' said, *"This is Jesus!"* . . . An' then the whole world grew bright. . . . An' I begun to feel sech a love in my soul as I never felt before. . . . An' then, all of a sudden, it stopped, an' I said, "Dar's de white folks that have abused you . . . an' abused your people—think of them!" But then there came another rush of love through my soul, an' I cried out loud—"Lord, Lord, I can love even de white folks!"[1]

From this encounter with Jesus, Isabella's life took a dramatic turn. While the love of Jesus enabled her to forgive her white masters, this former slave woman, barefoot and dressed in a cotton dress and kerchief, took on the New York court system and won back her children, who had been sold away from her. Next, she was reunited with her brother, who recounted the tragic death of her sister, causing her to embark on a lifelong advocacy for the rights of black people and women. Feeling a call to proclaim Jesus across the land, she left her New York home in 1843, taking the name *Sojourner Truth* to fit her calling. From New England to the Midwest she became a powerful presence for the causes of abolition and women's suffrage. In Akron, Ohio, in 1852, she gave her famous "Ain't I a Woman?" speech, in which she replied with these words to several pastors who had spoken against the rights of women:

Dat man ober dar say dat women needs to be helped into carriages. . . . Nobody eber helped *me* into carriages . . . !

And ain't *I* a woman? . . .

I have plowed and planted and gathered into barns . . . and no man could head me—and ain't *I* a woman? . . .

I have born'd five childrun and seen 'em mos' all sold off into slavery, and when I cried out with mother's grief, none but Jesus heard—and ain't *I* a woman? . . .

Den dey talks 'bout . . . intellect. Now, what's dat got to do with women's rights or [Negroes'] rights? If my cup won't hold but a pint, and yourn holds a quart, wouldn't ye be mean not to let me have my little half-measure full? . . .

Den dat little man in black dar . . . he say women can't have as much rights as man, 'cause Christ warn't a woman. Whar did your Christ come from? . . . From God and a woman! Man had nothing to do with him![2]

The audience was overwhelmed by the logic and magnetic power of this slender, aging, illiterate ex-slave in whom the love of freedom and the fruits of the Spirit shone so brightly.

For thirty more years—until her death in 1883 at the age of ninety—Sojourner Truth traveled the length and breadth of the land speaking and working for the rights of black people and women. She had every reason to yield to the works of the flesh—anger, enmity, strife, jealousy, quarrels, dissensions, factions (Galatians 5:20). Yet, redeemed by Jesus from a heart of bitterness, she instead devoted her life to a passion for freedom and the fruits of the Spirit—love, joy, peace, patience, kindness, generosity, faithfulness, gentleness, and self-control. No law could restrain such things (Galatians 5:22-23). She lived by the Spirit in her heart and was guided by the Spirit in her daily walk (Galatians 5:25). For freedom Christ had set her free. She stood firm and did not submit to a yoke of slavery (Galatians 5:1).

LESSON PLAN

Begin by distributing writing materials, reading off the key words on your list, and asking class members to write down a word or phrase they associate with each key word. Call for their responses as the words come up in the questions below, in order to engage class members in discussion of Scripture in terms of their own thinking.

Then, drawing on the commentary above and the material in the student book [pages 30–38], lead the class members in discussion using the questions below. If you prefer to lecture, you may wish to use the questions as the basis for your presentation.

(1) *In what ways do you feel that you are a new being in Christ?*

The new being is the person set free by Christ from bondage to sin and death. The student book describes God's grace as its source, love as its essence, and a new life as its fruit. Ask for class members' responses to the words *Spirit, joy, patience, kindness, compassion,* and *faithfulness.* Try to get beyond definitions or synonyms to experiences and feelings that reflect the new being. **When** do the class members experience joy? In **what ways** has the Spirit of God touched their lives? **What** makes them patient and kind? **What** keeps them faithful to Christ? For **what causes** do they feel passionate? Tell the story of Sojourner Truth's conversion and of the life that resulted from it. Share your experience, and invite others to do the same. Explain that the Galatians had a new birth under Paul's ministry but were being tempted to give this up and to return to slavery to the law.

(2) *What attitudes and behaviors do you associate with the four categories of self-indulgence mentioned in Galatians 5:19-21 and in the student book [pages 33–37]?*

The student book groups the fifteen works of the flesh into four categories—sexual excess, idolatry, contentiousness, and carousing. Ask for responses to the words *flesh, impurity, idolatry, sorcery, enmity, anger, dissension, carousing,* and others on your list. Share your responses to "prime the pump." Refer to the explanations in "Bible Background" above, but do not stop with intellectual exposition. Encourage the class members to speak of actual experiences with these attitudes and actions. Explain that these "works of the flesh" were tearing the Galatian churches apart.

Ask: *How does this behavior affect our churches? In what ways does it harm our witness and ministry? How can we prevent its impact on us—as individuals and as a church? What was Paul's remedy? How can we make sure that we are "guided by the Spirit" (Galatians 5:25)?*

(3) *"Why did Paul place so much stress on the church?"* [student book, page 37].

Paul established the churches of Galatia on his missionary journeys. He won both Jews and Gentiles to Christ, organized them into communities of faith, trained their leaders, and nurtured their growth in faith and discipleship. Since leaving them, he had been praying for their continued development and maturity. Then, due in part to the instigation of Judaizers, there was a falling away. Dissension, quarrels, impurities, idolatry, jealousy, envy, and other works of the flesh disrupted the faith, stability, and harmony of the churches about which Paul cared so deeply.

Paul stressed the church because he was grieving over its decline and hoping that it could be built up again. He urged the Galatians to cease the works of the flesh and to trust the Spirit's guidance to bring forth its fruits. Only thus would the church resume its growth in faith and discipleship, as well as in numbers.

Ask the class members for their responses to the words *generosity*, *gentleness*, *self-control*, and *peace*. Share insights on their meanings from "The Fruit of the Spirit" section in the student book [pages 37–38], from the "Bible Background" section in this teacher book, and from your reading of commentaries. Invite class members to cite instances from their lives and from the life of your congregation in which these attitudes and behaviors have been in evidence. If there is currently some instance of dissension, jealousy, or impurity in your congregation, share your feelings about that and compare your feelings to those of Paul.

(4) *"What are some benefits of this new freedom? Some dangers?"* [student book, page 33].

The student book emphasizes that the way to Christian freedom is to "become slaves to one another" (Galatians 5:13). The Christian life is motivated by love, not by obedience. We are free to follow the leading of the Spirit rather than legal requirements. We live under grace, not under law. We can "love God and do as we please." The Spirit will guide us to do the loving thing in our relationships and decisions. Of course, we must prayerfully discern the Spirit's leading and be willing to follow the often hard path to which God points us. It would be easier to have a rule book to cover every situation. The benefit of freedom is the joy of choosing to live a life of love. The drawback is that it is often tough and risky to do the genuinely loving thing.

Ask for responses to the words *fruit*, *yoke*, *slave*, *peace*, and *love*—especially for the experiences or mental images that members associate with these words. For example, for a tree to bear fruit, much pruning and fertilizing is required. A yoke suggests drudgery, but it also channels brute energy into productive teamwork. Sojourner Truth and her family were brutalized by slavery; but once she escaped to freedom, she willingly gave devoted service to the cause of Christ and her fellow sufferers. Peace is not the absence of conflict but a creative, dynamic equilibrium surging with potential. Love is caring enough to risk all for the sake of another. The benefits, or fruits, of freedom come from dedicating our lives, like Sojourner Truth, to following the guidance of the Spirit.

To close the session, invite class members to pray for forgiveness for instances of the works of the flesh in our lives and church, for the guidance of the Spirit, and for strength to manifest the fruits of Christian freedom in our daily walk. Conclude by singing together the hymn "Spirit of God, Descend Upon My Heart."

[1] Quoted in *Cloud of Witnesses*, edited by Jim Wallis and Joyce Hollyday (Orbis Books, *Sojourners* magazine, 1991); page 124.
[2] Quoted in *Cloud of Witnesses*; pages 127–28.

TRY ANOTHER METHOD

Tell the story of Sojourner Truth, and ask one class member to read aloud her "Ain't I a Woman?" speech. Discuss the following questions: *How did Sojourner Truth's life express the joy of Christian freedom? Which of the works of the flesh did she meet in the treatment she received? Which might she have been tempted to manifest? Which fruits of the Spirit do you see in her life? How do you assess the way she expressed her passion and what she achieved?*

Shift to a personal level by asking: *Have any of you been liberated from bondage (that is, from slavery to an inner or outer force, such as alcohol, debt, or abuse)? How did it feel to be enslaved? How were you freed? What was the response, in terms of feelings, choices, commitments, or lifestyle? What tempts us to give up our freedom and to "submit again to a yoke of slavery" (Galatians 5:1)? How can we be sure to "live by the Spirit . . . [and] also be guided by the Spirit" (Galatians 5:25)?*

Chapter Five

CHALLENGED TO LOVE

PURPOSE

To encourage us to nurture and support people, both within and without the community of faith, through the Spirit of Christ

BIBLE PASSAGE

Galatians 6:1-10, 14-18
Background: Galatians 6

> ### CORE VERSE
> Let us work for the good of all, and especially for those of the family of faith. (Galatians 5:10)

GET READY

Read through Galatians 6 in several translations. Consult commentaries on the passage, and read the article on "love" in one or more Bible dictionaries and word books.

Take a newspaper to the session to point to situations of need where Christian love could make a difference.

As this study comes to a close, think of the transitions life will inevitably bring in your church and in the lives of class members. Ask God to guide them so to internalize this chapter that they may face whatever comes in the spirit of love, bearing one another's burdens and working for the good of all (Galatians 6:2, 10).

BIBLE BACKGROUND

Paul concluded his appeal to the Galatians with some practical advice on Christian love. Followers of Jesus should be gentle and forgiving, help one another through the hard places, be humble, fulfill their duties, support their teachers, be faithful in good works, and promote the well-being of Christian and non-Christian alike. Paul reminded his readers that only Christ, and not circumcision (a symbol for the law), can bring about a new creation. It was for proclaiming this message of saving grace that Paul suffered, and he closed his letter with a blessing of this grace for his brothers and sisters in Christ.

Galatians 6:1. The emphasis on freedom in Chapter 5 led logically to the question of what to do with members who used freedom as license to engage in unchristian behavior. If we are liberated by Christ from rules and regulations, how do we deal with those who take advantage of this liberation? Paul's answer: Gently. He addressed, not the sinner, but the community, "the spiritual." He did not scold the wayward but rather counseled the faithful not to expel them from the community. Christians are to practice the fruits of the Spirit (Galatians 5:22-23) in aiding the backslider to return to the fold. They are also to be wary lest the sinful act or attitude (the works of the flesh in Galatians 5:19-21) of the unfaithful spread to others in the community.

Verse 2. A second piece of ethical advice had to do with the problem of individualism. A spirit of "do your own thing" had infected the churches. Apparently, people had been saying their own prayers, fulfilling their own duties, and observing their own standards of right—but not supporting and caring for one another.

The law of Christ—the law of love—demands that Christians help one another. We are to love our neighbor as ourselves (Matthew 22:39). Only by bearing one another's burdens can we fulfill Christ's intent. There is no such thing as a solitary Christian.

Verse 3. Third, Christians are called to careful self-examination. We are expected to acknowledge both our limitations and our gifts. Neither a false pride nor a false humility is helpful. We must neither pretend to be something we are not nor avoid responsibility by claiming lack of ability or knowledge. We may deceive ourselves through boasting and pretending but rarely do we deceive others. Denying our gifts may convince others, but inside we know we are holding back. Honest participation in the Christian community calls for rigorous, unassuming assessment of our strengths and shortcomings and finding the place of service for which we are best suited.

Verse 4. Personal responsibility was the next guideline Paul offered. Each of us must evaluate our own contribution. We cannot ride on our neighbor's coattails; neither can we measure our success by our neighbor's failure. The "then" that connects the two clauses of this verse is a reference to the Last Judgment. When we appear before God, we will have only our own work to present. The standard by which we will then be judged is whether we have manifested the fruits of the Spirit (Galatians 5:22-23). Paul was not advocating a self-serving pride but an honest recognition of our value to the community. He boasted only of "the cross of our Lord Jesus Christ" (Galatians 6:14) and expected the same of all Christians—including us. We are called to cultivate our God-given gifts, accept our responsibility for the work and well-being of the community, measure the effects of our efforts, and grow in confidence that we are workers who need not be ashamed (2 Timothy 2:15).

Verse 5. Fifth, we are to bear one another's burdens even while we carry our share of the load. We are not to depend on others for tasks we can do for ourselves nor are we to ask them to sustain the community while we look after our own interests. Responsible participation in the life of the community demonstrates that we are walking by the Spirit (Galatians 5:25). (See 1 Corinthians 12 and Ephesians 4:1-16 for descriptions of how the gifts of individuals build up the whole body of Christ.)

Verse 6. Paul next cited a specific example of the kind of mutual support and caring that should characterize the church. The teacher or pastor who nurtures a congregation in the Word deserves to be supported by those who benefit from these ministries. Jesus stated this principle as "the laborer deserves to be paid" (Luke 10:7). Certainly, the leader of a congregation should exemplify qualities of service and sacrifice—but so should every other Christian. A church should not exploit its pastor by expecting unstinting service while providing only meager compensation. "Those who are taught . . . must share in all good things with their teacher."

Verses 7-8. Paul joined the image of sowing and reaping with the contrast between flesh and spirit in Galatians 5:16-21 to remind us that in God's judgment our lives will be measured by how well they have expressed the fruits of the Spirit. Clarence Jordan paraphrased these verses this way: "Don't let anybody pull the wool over your eyes—you can't turn up your nose at God! For a person harvests exactly what he plants. If he plants the seed of materialism, he will reap the rottenness of materialism. And if he plants the seed of spirituality, he will harvest the superb life which the Spirit produces."[1]

Verse 9. So faithful discipleship is, in the long run, in our own best interest. Paul urged the Galatians not to lose heart but to keep plugging away at the tasks of mission and ministry to which they were called. Jordan put this as, "So let's not give up the good fight, for our harvest will come in its own good time if we keep on keeping on."[2]

Verse 10. With this hope of the triumph of righteousness beckoning us, Paul urged us to seize every opportunity to contribute to the well-being of others—not only our fellow Christians, but everyone in need. In the parable of the good Samaritan (Luke 10:25-37), Jesus made clear that our neighbor is not the person who lives next door or worships our way or speaks our language but rather the one in need. Paul reminded us that while deep love is shared in a community of faith, we are to "work for the good of all," regardless of their race, creed, color, or the degree of our affinity with them.

Verse 14. In verses 11-13 (which are omitted from our selection), after noting that he was writing this letter himself, Paul made one last argument against the Judaizers' efforts to lead the Galatians away from the gospel of grace. He contended that they were more interested in getting credit for winning converts than in the Galatians' spiritual well-being. Then Paul contrasted himself to these opponents by saying that while they gloried in numbers, he gloried in the cross. They spoke of their accomplishments; he spoke of what Christ had done for him. The cross—an instrument of cruel execution transformed into a symbol of divine love—turns everything upside down. As Paul had stated earlier (Galatians 2:19-21), his self was crucified with Christ so that he lived, not in the flesh, but by faith. The attractions of the world—fame, fortune, achievement, comfort, safety, position—no longer appealed to him.

Verse 15. It does not matter whether one is Jew or Gentile (circumcised or uncircumcised; see Galatians 3:28 and 5:6). What matters is that one is a new creature in Christ Jesus (2 Corinthians 5:17). A new power is available to overcome sin—"Christ who lives in me" (Galatians 2:20). The world is hostile to the reign of God, but in the cross its power has been defeated and its slaves set free. Christ has redeemed us from the "elemental spirits of the world" (Galatians 4:3-7), and in his Spirit we can bear different fruit (Galatians 5:22-24). The new creation is not just an inner change but the manifestation of the power of God in the world as a whole.

Verse 16. Paul proclaimed God's peace and mercy on all who obey God's rule. The new Israel includes both Jew and Gentile—all who accept the reign of God and who believe that God's grace frees them from the law and its demands.

Verse 17. Before giving his final blessing, Paul told his opponents not to bother him anymore. Like the Roman slaves and soldiers branded with the sign of those they served, so his body bore the marks of a servant of the Crucified One—of torture and persecution for his faith. Paul had suffered for Christ. What were their credentials by comparison?

Verse 18. The blessing with which the letter ends is similar to the blessings in Philippians 4:23 and Philemon 25. The addition of "brothers and sisters" lifts up the quality of community. "Your spirit" emphasizes the inner life; and "grace" is the central message of the whole letter—the unconditional love of God received by faith, which undercuts the need for the law.

INTRODUCE OUR NEED

Ken Imbody (not his real name) is one man whose life has been devoted to "nurturing and supporting people, both within and without the community of faith, through the Spirit of Christ." Converted at age eleven in a revival meeting, his faith was nurtured in a series of summer youth camps as well as in worship services and youth activities in his local church. As a young man he worked as a teacher and also as a grocery store clerk in his hometown, during which time he was active in his church.

Ken remembers being opposed to hunting animals and participating in war, but he was drafted for military service in World War II. He told me that he felt sympathetic with the Germans as they came in to surrender—"bedraggled, dirty, tired, worn out, defeated, wounded. Somehow you come to believe that the enemy is some kind of beast. But I still viewed them as human beings."

Ken kept his sensitivity and compassion as he took a position in a university placement office where he was able to find jobs for many needy and deserving people. Then he bought a rooming house on campus and devoted ten years to being landlord, support system, and listening ear for a succession of students. During this time he returned home on weekends to look after his aging parents and held a variety of church offices, including treasurer.

While Ken's parents were confined to a nursing home, he spent so much time there helping informally that the patients began calling him "Doc." After both his parents died, Ken, still single, sold his rooming house, entered nurse's training, then moved back to his hometown and became a nurse. He soon organized a campaign to build a new, modern nursing home and expressed his Christian care for persons by nursing there for several years.

Ken's church involvement led him into mission, and he went on a work team to Haiti. There he came face to face with massive human suffering and was so moved that he went back year after year—six weeks at a time. When I talked with him, Ken was seventy and had decided to retire from nursing and to volunteer to go to Haiti to work in Grace Children's Hospital.

Ken Imbody's compassion for suffering people and his concern to serve them, both within and outside the church, had been expressed in military service, college administration, student housing, nursing home care, and mission service. Commenting on this lifetime of "bearing one another's burdens," Ken told me, "I see it as an opportunity to be of help to people—somebody, anybody. Some kind of Christian work is what I want to do. The picture of retirement where the guy just putters around and grows flowers, takes his wife shopping, and plays shuffleboard and pinochle is not for me. I feel an obligation to do something. I guess that's stewardship. So you can see what kind of a character I am."

Whether he realized it or not, Ken had been responding to Galatians 6:9-10: "So let us not grow weary in doing what is right, for we will reap at harvest time, if we do not give up. So then, whenever we have an opportunity, let us work for the good of all, and especially for those of the family of faith."

LESSON PLAN

Introduce this session by writing the word *Love* on a chalkboard or large piece of paper and asking class members to share thoughts and experiences that this word calls to mind. Present the meanings of the Greek words for love given in the student book and other ideas gleaned from Bible dictionaries and word books. Explain that Christian love is the basis for the moral advice that Paul gave the Galatians in his closing chapter.

Then, drawing on the commentary above and the material in the student book [pages 39–47], lead the class members in discussion using the questions below. If you prefer to lecture, you may wish to use the questions as the basis for your presentation.

(1) *"What kinds of love have affected you? In what ways?"* [student book, page 42].

As a starter, note the class members' responses to the word *love*. Examples could include parental love, forgiving love, marital love, the love of friendship, puppy love, compassionate love, tough love, the love that takes risks, suffering love, sacrificial love, the love of comrades, and the love that goes the second mile. The effects of these kinds of love can be to help us grow, to force us to change, to heal our wounds both physical and emotional, to reconcile relationships, to support us in difficult times, to motivate us to do our best, to lead us to repent, to call forth our gifts, to teach us to love in return, and to foster solidarity and partnership. Invite the class members to share examples in their lives of each of these.

(2) *"What differences do you see between agape love and that practiced by most people today?"* [student book, page 43].

Explain that *agape* is self-giving love that puts the well-being of others ahead of self, even to the point of giving one's life. Ask for examples of this love in the life of Jesus and among people you know or have heard of. Jesus' healings of the sick, lame, and demented; his forgiveness of sinners; his compassion for the poor and oppressed; and his death on the cross could be mentioned.

Persons who gave their life for a cause, like Archbishop Romero and Martin Luther King, Jr.; persons who devoted their lives to serving others, like Ken

Imbody and Mother Teresa; persons who risked their lives to save someone from drowning or from a burning building; and persons who sacrificed their own time or opportunity for the sake of another, like mothers and teammates, could be lifted up. Ask the class members for examples. The difference between this self-giving love and the more typical expressions of love is basically that we usually expect to get something in return when we love and soon stop giving if there is nothing in it for us. We may even stop loving God if our prayers are not answered the way we want.

(3) *"How do you feel when you see persons failing to keep what you believe to be God's standards? What should you do?"* [student book, page 45].

The student book interprets Paul's admonition that "all must carry their own loads" (Galatians 6:5) to mean that "each must answer to his or her own conscience." That is, we must not judge others for not meeting the standards we believe God requires of us. Judgment belongs to God, not to us; our role is to support, encourage, and be patient with one another.

When someone ignores or rejects God's will, we may feel angry, resentful, self-righteous, impatient, betrayed, let down, or deserted. Our response should be tailored to the circumstances and to the feelings and needs of the other. Approaches could include offers of support, encouragement, assistance, and forgiveness; we should be willing to extend another chance. Also useful, however, could be a rebuke, a challenge to do better, a call to accountability, or a reminder of who and whose the offenders are and of the covenants they have broken. Repeated willful disregard for the promises they have made would call for ever sterner measures. You may wish to have the class members discuss situations known to most of them and how these could be handled in ways that give expression to the fruits of the Spirit and the law of love.

(4) *"To what good are you drawn? How is your interest realized?"* [student book, page 46].

The student book poses this question after stressing that in Galatians 6:10, Paul commissioned us to express God's love through service to Christian and non-Christian alike. Ask the class members to name the areas of need in church, community, and world where we **could** help if we just **would**. Ask class members to share what needs they are personally drawn to, and have people tell what they have done and are doing because of their interest. Read aloud headlines from the newspaper you have brought to the session, and ask what class members could do to help in each situation.

To close the session, have a time of silent prayer, asking the class members to meditate on the question, "Are you motivated toward good?" Invite class members to pray for God's forgiveness for times they have known they could do good and have not done it, for vision and sensitivity to see the opportunity and need, and for strength to respond by "working for the good of all." Conclude this prayer time by having the class members sing either "Lord, Whose Love Through Humble Service" or "Open My Eyes."

[1] From *The Cotton Patch Version of Paul's Epistles,* by Clarence Jordan (Association Press, 1968); page 103.
[2] From *The Cotton Patch Version of Paul's Epistles;* page 103.

TRY ANOTHER METHOD

Briefly review all the chapters in this study of Galatians. They can be summarized as follows:

Chapter 1, "Delivered From Bondage" (Galatians 1:6-7; 2:11-21): We are challenged to live in the freedom that the gospel of Christ offers us.

Chapter 2, "Adopted as God's Children" (Galatians 3:1-5, 23–4:7): Adoption into God's family makes us all equally children of God.

Chapter 3, "Freed to Grow" (Galatians 4:8-20): We struggle in our spiritual journeys between growing in grace and turning back.

Chapter 4, "Enabled to Bear Fruit" (Galatians 5:1, 13-26): We are called to express the joy of Christian freedom in the fruits of the Spirit.

Chapter 5, "Challenged to Love" (Galatians 6:1-10, 14-18): We are to care for all people, both in and out of the church, in the spirit of Christ.

List this summary on a chalkboard or on a large piece of paper. Then ask class members to recall ideas, illustrations, Scripture verses, or moments in the sessions while studying this material that have been particularly meaningful. Write the responses alongside the appropriate Scripture and theme for each chapter.